Wicked

MONMOUTH COUNTY

Wicked

MONMOUTH COUNTY

GEORGE JOYNSON

Charleston — London

THE
History
PRESS

Published by The History Press
Charleston, SC 29403
www.historypress.net

Front cover images: New Jersey State Police Museum, Crook family descendants, John A. and
Virginia Woolley, Donald Voorhees and the Red Bank Library.
Back cover images: John A. and Virginia Woolley, Rue family descendants and Ocean
Township Police Department.

First published 2010

Manufactured in the United States

ISBN 978.1.59629.997.9

Library of Congress Cataloging-in-Publication Data

Joynson, George.
Wicked Monmouth County / George Joynson.
p. cm.
Includes bibliographical references and index.
ISBN 978-1-59629-997-9
1. Crime--New Jersey--Monmouth County--Case studies. 2. Crime--New Jersey--
Monmouth County--History--20th century. 3. Detectives--New Jersey--Monmouth County-
-Case studies. I. Title.
HV6795.M63J69 2010
363.25092'274946--dc22
2010022980

Contents

CONTENTS

Introduction

W ho can resist a bright red blinking sign that screams "Breaking News!" without wondering what it has to say? A hundred years ago, front-page newspaper headlines did exactly that. Reporters presented the scandalous details of the murder of fisherman John Woolley in Spring Lake, the thrilling minute-by-minute account of capturing escaped criminal Ginger Ayers in Little Silver and the sensational ongoing "crime of the century," Charles Lindbergh's baby's kidnapping. The people are long gone, but the marks they made in history remain. Reading the writers' passionate accounts in black and white print of yesteryear is like reliving every minute. Back then, their enthusiasm was obvious in their choice of words. Exciting events in print are captured for all time. You can't help getting a strong sense of being there, as if it just happened yesterday.

Wicked Monmouth County revisits law and order in the early 1900s through the lives of three men. Monmouth County Detectives Jacob Rue, William Mustoe and Harry Crook investigated local crime, from high-profile murder cases to horse thieves and corner loafers. These civil servants put men behind bars and sent two to the gallows. This book visits their human side. Follow the events in the lives of these three men from their early years to retirement, as they sometimes achieved success and sometimes suffered through failure and tragedy.

While all three were at times proficient and effective on the job, only Mustoe retired with a clean record. Captain Mustoe's career in law enforcement lasted thirty-six years. Detective Rue tested the thin line that separates cops from criminals, and Chief Crook fought gangland crime during the Prohibition Era before yielding to temptation.

People of the early 1900s lived through the *Titanic*, *Morro Castle* and *Hindenburg* disasters, World War I, the Roaring Twenties, the Great Depression and Prohibition. They experienced the transition from horse and buggy to Ford's Model T (which cost $345 in 1916) and from silent movies to talkies. The lives of these three detectives will take you on a journey through local history, through law and order and chaos.

Section One
Detective Jacob B. Rue Jr.
(1873-1933)

Rue's Early Years

On five separate occasions, Jacob B. Rue Jr. resigned from his job. On six separate occasions, he found himself the defendant in a lawsuit. Jacob Rue wasn't afraid to quit, and he wasn't afraid to speak his mind. He stood up for what he believed. He took action, and he did so without fear of consequence or what others thought of him.

In 1923, while working the Santaniello murder case, Detective Rue publicly criticized his coworker. Rue said, "The murderers in this case probably will never be found, due to the inefficiency of Detective Charles O. Davenport." Not the nicest thing to say in public about his co-worker, but on this occasion Rue was right about one thing: this case would never be solved. To this day, no one has ever been arrested for the murder of Salvatore Santaniello, the bootlegger from New York City.

With fiery determination, Jacob, alias Jake, alias J.B., got the job done the best way he knew how. Rue journeyed through several careers in his lifetime. He started as an avid horseman and stable owner. He created the biggest auto repair garage and boat yard in Monmouth County and then tried his hand as a local theater owner. He served the people of Red Bank as constable, marshal and chief of police. Twice he was employed as a Monmouth County detective, and for a while he headed up his own private detective agency. Throughout, J.B. seemed to be in the center of excitement wherever he ventured.

Rue had a few scrapes with the law in his early years. After paying a steep fine for a bribery conviction, Rue stayed on the good side of the law throughout the rest of his life. He made many arrests during his years as

Jacob Bergen Rue Jr. *Courtesy Rue family.*

a detective. Besides arsonists, horse thieves, forgers and other felons, Detective Rue arrested several men on first-degree murder charges. Prosecutors in Monmouth County assigned him to investigate more than a dozen high-profile murders, and Rue testified at some of these trials.

Jacob Rue left a vivid paper trail from the activities and events he got involved in, and the image history makes of Rue is not of a person who would wait around for things to happen. Rue was a doer. Right or wrong, Jacob Rue made things happen. He was a tall man, of medium build, with blue eyes and brown hair.

Jacob Bergen Rue Jr. was born September 12, 1873, in Freehold, Monmouth County, New Jersey, to parents Jacob Bergen Rue Sr. and Adeline Conover Rue. His middle name came from his paternal grandmother, Margaret Bergen. Jacob was their third child, having an elder brother Joseph and sister Drusilla. When he was born, the Rue family lived on a 158-acre farm along Colts Neck Turnpike, about a half mile east of Freehold, with three domestic servants. His father, Jacob B. Rue Sr., founded the First National Bank of Freehold.

In 1856, Mr. Rue gave $50,000 to the bank as working capital and was appointed cashier. The bank officers promoted Rue to president when the bank incorporated. He held that position for twenty years before retiring in 1883. At the Rue homestead, Mr. Rue allowed Auctioneer Jacob Shutts to hold auctions in his barns. Shutts auctioned off personal property for several large estates. It must have been exciting for young Jacob to watch the horses, wagons and harnesses coming in and the high bidders leaving with their purchases.

Jacob's great-grandfather, John Rue, was a Patriot in the Revolutionary War. John Rue served as a private in Captain John Walton's troop in the

Detective Jacob B. Rue Jr. (1873–1933)

Rue's father, president of First National Bank of Freehold, Jacob B. Rue Sr. (1827–1885). History of Monmouth County, New Jersey, *Ellis, 467.*

Light Dragoons of Monmouth, New Jersey. Dragoons were trained infantry men mounted on horses.

At the age of five, young Jacob and his family moved to Red Bank, where he began attending public school. Jacob was in eighth grade when his father died of heart disease on March 19, 1885. His father's death happened suddenly and unexpectedly while the family was on vacation in Jacksonville, Florida.

In the 1880s, Jacksonville was a popular winter resort for wealthy northern families. The Rues had left Freehold on February 9, when Mr. Rue seemed ordinarily vigorous and cheerful, with plans to return in the spring. Mr. Rue was described as a warm and reliable friend and an affectionate husband and father. During his long and successful business career as a bank president, he was just and fair in his dealings, but at times people perceived him as brusque and preemptory in his manner. He was frank in his expressions and had a reputation for hating scammers. Mr. Rue was described as quick-witted and made his decisions with clear and precise logic. Young Jacob was just twelve years old when his father died.

AN EARLY INTEREST IN HORSES AND SPEED

One day in 1892, when he was still a teenager, Jake was driving his horse and buggy at a rapid and unsafe speed down Broad Street in Red Bank when he ran into William P. Corlies. The elderly Mr. Corlies did not see Rue coming. The shaft of Rue's carriage struck Corlies in the side and knocked him to the ground. Corlies was badly bruised and shaken up. They took him to Dr. Jeremiah Sayre's office, but luckily, he suffered no broken bones.

Rue liked riding horses and going fast. A few months later, he entered his horse Boston in a half-mile race along the Tinton Falls Turnpike versus Henry Hendrickson's horse All Brown. Hendrickson hired a rider, but Rue rode his own mount. Boston was the favorite and led at the beginning but bolted at the quarter pole, allowing All Brown to win easily. The race attracted a large crowd, with many betting on the outcome. After the race, Hendrickson put All Brown up for auction with a starting bid of $25.00. It didn't take long for bidders to realize that Rue had to have the fastest horse in town. Rue won All Brown with a high bid of $32.50.

Broad Street, Red Bank, 1890s. *Courtesy Red Bank Library Historic Photograph Collection.*

Detective Jacob B. Rue Jr. (1873–1933)

Horseman Jacob B. Rue Jr. *Courtesy Red Bank Library Historic Photograph Collection.*

Two weeks after the race, Rue bought another horse from Edward Bennett, paying him partly in cash and using a promissory note to pay the remaining fifteen dollars in ninety days. When Rue didn't pay the note, Bennett sued him. Just twenty years old, this was Rue's first court appearance, and it did not go well. Justice of the Peace Charles Cothren issued a judgment for nonpayment in Bennett's favor. Bennett placed a levy on Rue's horse, buggy and harness, but Rue sold the horse and outfit to Tinton Falls Constable Aaron Tilton. Tilton then sold it to Frank Watts for five dollars, and then Watts sold it to James Walsh. Bennett brought suit against Walsh and was able to recover the horse and buggy, but the saddle got misplaced along the way.

Jacob Rue and his buddy Charlie Applegate got into trouble one day in February 1893 when, after imbibing liberal amounts of liquor, they mounted their horses and played cowboy down the streets of Red Bank. Still single but not for much longer, Rue and his pal Charlie were out to have a good time. With unbounded enthusiasm, the two young bloods rode their ponies slipshod along Monmouth Avenue. Hootin' and hollerin', they let their imaginations run wild as they pretended to herd cattle, tame bucking broncos and go on a long buffalo hunt down Maple Avenue. Marshal Patrick Hackett and Frank Fielder finally corralled the two and took them before

A confident pose. Young Anna Throckmorton Conover married Jacob Rue in 1893. *Courtesy Rue family.*

Justice of the Peace Cothren, who fined them five dollars each for their disruptive cavortings. The boys were not using firearms, but Justice Cothren warned that if they tried this trick again, their fine would be considerably larger.

On August 1, 1893, Jacob married Anna Throckmorton Conover. On his marriage license, Rue listed his occupation as speculator. Nine months later, they enjoyed the birth of their first child, a son they named Jacob Bergen Rue III, born in Manhattan, New York City. The Throckmorton and Conover families have deep ancestral roots in Monmouth County, dating back to the early formation of the county in the 1660s. John Throckmorton was among the first lot owners of Middletown Township.

STOUTWOOD STABLES

Rue further advanced his interest in horses when he purchased the Stoutwood Stables on Maple Avenue from William H. Conklin. The name Stoutwood came from John W. Stout, who built an oval trotting track on his farm and called it Stoutwood Park. In the fall of 1895, Rue advertised Stoutwood Stables as having the best horses and equipment available. Rue, now a young married man with children in his first business venture, must have been very excited. "I bought Stoutwood Stables!" his advertisement proclaimed.

In the 1890s, horse and wagon was the most common means of travel over dirt and dusty roads. Livery stables were a competitive market, much like

I've Bought The Stoutwood Stables

and have added a number of new rigs to the stock, among them being a coupé and a team of black cobs, which make the finest looking turnout in town. I don't sell or exchange, and therefore know if my horses have any bad tricks; if they have I won't keep them. When I give a lady a horse and say it is safe for her to drive it—it is.

Stoutwood Stables,
Next to Central Hotel.

J. B. RUE, Proprietor.

The Pleasure of Driving

is increased ten-fold by perfect satisfaction. Perfect satisfaction consists mainly of good health, good weather and a stylish horse and wagon. Look out for your own health, let Providence supply the weather, and come here for your turnout.

I have natty road wagons, stylish buggies and two seated single and double rigs. I have good driving horses, stylish horses; horses that women can drive with perfect safety.

Few private rigs have the style about them that mine have.

Stoutwood Stables,
Next to Central Hotel.

J. B. RUE, Proprietor.

Above, left: "I've Bought the Stoutwood Stables." Advertisement for Rue's first business venture. Red Bank Register, *October, 16, 1895.*

Above, right: "The Pleasure of Driving." Rue's advertisement for his Stoutwood Stables. Red Bank Register, *October 30, 1895.*

today's car dealerships. Rue got the idea to initiate an aggressive marketing campaign to attract female customers. He claimed he had natty wagons, stylish buggies and "horses that women can drive with perfect safety." He had horses for hire with rigs that were clean and polished. His strategy worked, although he may have regretted it.

A month after he purchased the business, Rue filed a complaint against one of his young female customers, Miss Cora Knapp from New York, for abusing one of his horses. Cora was the daughter of the prominent Knapp family of New York. On Rue's complaint, police arrested Miss Knapp, and a hearing was scheduled before Justice of the Peace Henry Childs. The case was never heard, as Knapp settled with Rue out of court for undisclosed terms. Miss Knapp was back in court on another matter in January 1896, when she sued her fiancé, Robert Tappen of Long Branch, in Supreme Court for breach of promise of marriage, for $25,000.

Unfortunately, a devastating fire broke out at Rue's stables in January 1896. Eleven horses died in the blazing inferno. Fire destroyed the contents of his stables, including eight wagons, several carriages, sleighs, harnesses and other gear. Edward Haley was coming home from a dance when he saw the flames and gave the alarm. Henry Hendrickson, who worked for Rue and lived nearby, was the first to arrive. Hendrickson broke down the stable door and led two ponies belonging to the United States Express Company to safety. By then the building was in massive flames. Nearby, a conductor for the Southern Railroad saw the flames and kept blowing his train whistle. Someone rang the uptown gong, but the downtown gong failed to work

Rue's Stoutwood Stables was conveniently located right next to Central Hotel. *Courtesy Randall Gabrielan.*

properly. By the time the firemen arrived, it was too late to save the building. They turned their hoses onto the Central Hotel and William Applegate's house adjoining Rue's burning stables. The firefighters did an excellent job of preventing the fire from spreading to the other buildings.

The cause of the fire was a mystery. Rue said he left the stables about 11:00 p.m. that night. He said no one slept there and no one had entered there. He estimated damages to be about $22,000 but was insured for half that amount. Nothing except ashes and the shell of a building remained. It became a curiosity for passersby. The loss caused Rue some financial difficulties.

Red Bank Commissioner Obadiah E. Davis appointed Rue chief of police. *Courtesy Red Bank Library Historic Photograph Collection.*

Despite this tragic event, Rue pressed on. Undeterred by the setback, he purchased a fifty-foot by one-hundred-foot lot on White Street next to Harrison Woodward's Blacksmith Shop. Rue hired Obadiah E. Davis to build a two-story livery stable on his lot at a cost of $1,900. Two years later, Rue sold his stable to Frank A. Schultz for $7,500, who later sold to Robert T. Smith.

NEW JERSEY NATIONAL GUARD

Private Rue trained with the Monmouth Cavalry Troop, New Jersey National Guard, under First Sergeant Howard Whitfield at the Sea Girt Encampment, July 18–25, 1896. Rue won several medals for marksman and sharpshooter with his proficiency handling weapons. By 1904, Rue reached the rank of first sergeant.

When the Spanish-American War of 1898 broke out, Reverend Charles H. Jones of Newark paid Rue $125 for a horse. Rue told Reverend Jones that he would pay him $100 if he returned the horse when the war was over. To Rue's surprise, the war lasted only a few months. It was a costly miscalculation. After serving in the Second New Jersey Volunteer Infantry, Company G, the reverend returned the horse, but Rue refused to pay. Reverend Jones brought suit; Rue settled before the hearing and paid him the $100.

Private Rue, *third from left*, behind First Sergeant Howard Whitfield, trained with the Monmouth Cavalry Troop, New Jersey National Guard, at Camp Sea Girt for two weeks in July 1896. *Courtesy Red Bank Library Historic Photograph Collection.*

Detective Jacob B. Rue Jr. (1873–1933)

Rue obviously showed some leadership qualities. By 1904, he had reached the rank of first sergeant, indicated by the three stripes and diamond on his sleeve. The hook on his belt held a saber. *Courtesy Rue family.*

Later, Rue purchased an expensive racing mare named Lottie M. from Augustus Chandler, former mayor of Long Branch. In 1906, $450 was a large amount of money to pay for a racehorse. In 1907, Rue sold his trotter, Walter E., to Joseph Hance. Rue had owned the horse about three years. It had a track record of 2:22½.

TROUBLE WITH
THE LAW

The 1890s, described by Mark Twain, was a profitable era marked by crime. The Panic of 1893 set off a statewide economic depression, with railroads and banks filing for bankruptcy. It was under these tough economic conditions, together with the personal losses of his stable fire, that Rue ran into more legal and financial troubles three years into his marriage. On March 28, 1896, Jacob borrowed $300 from Asher B. Holmes and signed a note promising to pay in ninety days.

Holmes was not the kind of person to cross. The Western Union Telegraph Company once erected a telegraph pole on the front of his property, which he did not like. In less than a week, Holmes chopped it down.

Rue's competition, an advertisement from Birdsall & Son. Red Bank Register, *January 13, 1904.*

When Rue did not honor the note, Holmes sued him for nonpayment of principal and interest, asking for twice the amount. Rue hired Attorney John T. Russell for defense, but in September, Judge J. Clarence Conover of Monmouth County Common Pleas ruled in favor of Holmes. Judge Conover ordered Rue to pay damages, interest and court costs totaling $336.47.

The next month, Amos Birdsall and his son Percival sued Rue for $743.50 in damages. Birdsall & Son owned stables on Monmouth Street that sold carriages and harnesses and competed directly with Rue's stables. For the past six months, Rue had been buying livery stable supplies from the Birdsalls, including a Brougham harness, a Babcock spindle, several buggies and other supplies on contract with a three-month promissory note. Again, the judge ruled against defendant Rue by default, ordering him to pay the full amount owed plus another $35.39 for court costs.

Rue's troubles were more serious the next year, when he was indicted on two separate charges. Rue was charged with assault and battery on Murray Bodine but was found not guilty on June 25, 1897. Bodine was a member of the Monmouth Boat Club, a boisterous character known for drinking heavily and for wearing a buffalo robe while doing a bear dance at the club's smokers. A week later, Rue was back in court facing charges of conspiracy. Conspiracy is a serious offense, when a partnership is formed for criminal intent.

Conspiracy Charges

Red Bank Constable James Walsh arrested Jacob Rue and J. Frank Patterson for conspiracy and took them to Freehold. On January 20, 1897, Monmouth County Prosecutor Wilbur A. Heisley charged Rue with blackmailing restaurateur John Carroll. Carroll owned a restaurant in the opera house block of Red Bank. His complaint stated that Rue and Patterson told him they had evidence that he sold liquor illegally on New Year's Eve. Rue and Patterson told Carroll that they had fourteen people who would swear to it. They told him that if he didn't pay them hush money, they would go to the grand jury. Carroll gave them $5.00 cash and a check for $7.50 and then turned them in.

Rue denied the charges as totally false and said he would sue everybody involved. Patterson resigned his job as sergeant-at-arms for the Monmouth County Courts, a position he had held for fourteen years. Both pled not guilty.

J. Frank Patterson, convicted of conspiracy, was later appointed chief of police. *Courtesy Red Bank Library Historic Photograph Collection.*

The indictment claimed that Patterson and Rue "wickedly, falsely, fraudulently and unlawfully conspired, and with intent, agreed to cheat and maliciously defraud John Carroll." Rue posted $3,000 bail and was released on his own recognizance. He hired attorneys Joseph Rielly and R. TenBroeck Stout for defense. Rielly immediately filed a motion to quash, but Judge Conover denied it. The case came to trial in the Monmouth County Courthouse in Freehold on July 1, 1897.

Detective Jacob B. Rue Jr. (1873–1933)

Jurors in *State of New Jersey v. Rue and Patterson*
Monmouth County Courthouse, Freehold, New Jersey
July 1, 1897

Louis N. Cook	Joseph T. Hendrickson	Leonard J. Arrowsmith
James Bray Jr.	Charles H. Boud	William C. Buck
John A. Smock	Joseph Rue	Frederick Eckert
Albert Sickles	Edward Boone	Jefferson Ackerson

Rue and Patterson's trial lasted two days. Carroll took the stand on the first day but would not answer any of Prosecutor Heisley's questions about selling liquor illegally for fear of incriminating himself. Overnight, Carroll had a change of heart. The next day, Carroll returned to the witness stand and told all. After a three-hour session, the jury found both Patterson and Rue guilty of conspiracy as charged.

Judge Conover sentenced Patterson to pay a $500 fine plus court costs and Rue to pay a $400 fine plus costs. Rue appealed to a higher court, which upheld the lower court ruling, and he promptly paid his fine. His fine was equal to about a year's salary. Patterson couldn't come up with enough money and went to jail for a term equal to one day for each dollar he owed.

On July 21, Rue arrested Carroll for selling liquor illegally. Carroll was taken before Justice Sickles and posted bail. While Carroll's arrest following Rue's conviction seemed a bit revengeful on Rue's part, Rue was now working with the law on his side. Rue's conspiracy conviction had a profound impact on him. It was the last time he was on the wrong side of the law—a huge turning point in his life. From then on, Rue lived in an honorable way.

Career on the Good Side

A t the turn of the twentieth century, Jacob Rue was living with his wife, Anna T., son Jacob, daughter Margaret, widowed mother-in-law, Mrs. Ann Marie Conover, and two female servants at 43 West Front Street in the Red Bank section of Shrewsbury Township, New Jersey.

It was about this time that Rue's law enforcement career began to take shape in the right direction. Once on the good side, Rue never looked back. In the summer of 1899, Red Bank Commissioner Obadiah Davis appointed Rue as the township's assistant marshal. It was a position without pay, but Rue accepted. On November 15, 1899, Assistant Marshal Rue made his first major arrest.

THE JAMES WALSH MURDER

Upon receiving word that William Bullock was being held in South Amboy, Assistant Marshal Jacob Rue and Police Chief Franklin Stryker boarded the 3:00 a.m. northbound freight train in Red Bank. At South Amboy, the two officers of the law took charge of their prisoner and returned by the newspaper train to Freehold, where they proceeded to lock Bullock up in the county jail. Bullock was charged with the first-degree murder of James Walsh, former Red Bank chief of police. Rue was just twenty-six years old when he had the responsibility of taking custody of his first alleged murderer.

Left: Rue's young daughter, Margaret Rue, at Christmas in 1897. *Monmouth County Historical Association Library & Archives.*

Below: Rue's grown-up daughter, Margaret, on horseback, circa 1919. *Courtesy Red Bank Library Historic Photograph Collection.*

Detective Jacob B. Rue Jr. (1873–1933)

Drawing of escaped convicted murderer William Bullock appeared on the front page. Freehold Transcript, *September 14, 1900.*

Red Bank Chief of Police Franklin P. Stryker. *Courtesy Red Bank Library Historic Photograph Collection.*

On November 13, 1899, Walsh was serving two summonses to Bullock, one for damages to John Stillwell's wagon and harness and the other for nonpayment of his debt owed to Robert Allen Jr. of $5. William Bullock was having legal and money problems and objected. The men began to argue. When Walsh said, "I want you to go with me," Bullock refused.

"No, I won't go." Walsh insisted that he had to go with him.

"I will take you with me if I have to take you dead!"

Bullock relented and said that if he must go, he would, if he could just go in the house for a moment. Bullock went inside and put on a second pair of pants. When he came out, he pulled a revolver and shot Walsh three times, killing him instantly. Then Bullock fled.

Walsh was born about 1829 at Newcastle Upon Tyne, England, and came to the United States as a young boy with his mother. During the gold rush, he mined in the California gold fields for sixteen years and then moved to Red Bank in 1870. His wife and three children survived him.

William Bullock was a married African American farmhand and had a young daughter. His large frame, dark black skin and three gold-capped teeth made him easily identifiable. He paid fifty cents to be rowed across the Shrewsbury River, hopped unnoticed into the back of a farmer's wagon heading north and then walked the rest of the way to the Matawan Train Station. Workers in Matawan noticed him board the train and notified police. At the South Amboy Train Station, Police Officer James McDonald was there waiting for him.

Back in Red Bank, Coroner William E. MacDonald held an inquest into the death of James Walsh, at which Rue testified. Under oath, Rue said, "I asked Mr. Bullock if he had any intention of killing Mr. Walsh. I asked him if he went in the house to get his gun and at the same time put his pants on, if his intentions were to kill Mr. Walsh and he said yes." While in Rue's custody, Bullock talked freely about his feelings toward Walsh. Coroner MacDonald asked Rue what he had said in that regard. Rue replied, "He said he thought he was hounding him and prosecuting him, and he didn't know any other way; he put the extra pants on because he thought he would be out all night." The coroner's report concluded that "James Walsh met his death at the hands of one William Bullock, on November 13, 1899, about 4:00 p.m., at 198 Stout Street, East Red Bank, New Jersey, being shot four times by a pistol here in evidence and three bullets taken from the body." Bullock pled not guilty in self-defense, but the jury didn't buy it.

At Bullock's trial, Judge Gilbert Collins sentenced him "to hang by the neck until he be dead." A week before the scheduled execution, Bullock's lawyer presented new evidence and convinced the Court of Errors and Appeals to order a new trial. Bullock boasted that he would never hang.

While he was waiting for the new trial, Bullock escaped from jail. He broke a hole in the cement floor of his jail cell, which led to a passageway, and then squeezed through a hole under the foundation of the jail walls. How he got an iron chisel no one knew. Why no one heard him hammering no one knew. Who dug the foundation exit from the outside no one knew. With help from persons unknown, Bullock found his way to freedom and was never again seen in Monmouth County. Sheriff Davis telegraphed a $500 reward for his capture.

Bullock's freedom didn't last long. In December 1900, lumberman E. Garrett recognized Bullock in a store near Portsmouth, Virginia, and told him he was taking him in for the reward. Bullock refused and made a mad dash. Garrett shot and killed him and collected the reward but faced murder charges in so doing. Back home in Red Bank, Assistant Marshal Rue continued to keep the peace and enforce the laws.

Wheelmen Hauled In

In 1901, the Red Bank commissioners appointed Rue as marshal of Red Bank, but Rue lasted less than three weeks at his new position. One night during his reign, the zealous new marshal arrested seven bicyclers for riding at night without lights. Rue's first "collar" was Patrick Murphy of Fair Haven. Murphy claimed he was unaware of the ordinance, so Justice Henry Childs waived the $5.00 fine but charged him $1.50 costs. Then Rue brought in John Dowling and his brother James, and then Charles Lewis, all of Fair Haven. Rumblings began circulating in the courtroom that Rue was only arresting out-of-town people. Five minutes later, Rue returned with George Cooper, a civil engineer of Red Bank, and John Mouser of Herbert Street. Justice Childs waived all their fines and charged them only the costs due the justice and marshal.

Editor John B. Cook of the *Red Bank Register* wrote that the arrests made by Marshal Rue were "an indignation" to townspeople. There was a law on the books requiring lights on bicycles at night, but the rule had not been strictly enforced. Sometimes an officer would give a warning, but until then none had made any arrests. Rather than making Red Bank a better place, Cook wrote that Rue's arrests would encourage others to stay away from town. Cook complained that Rue was unfit to hold any official position in town.

Five days after Cook published his scolding opinion, Rue resigned. Obviously, Rue didn't like the criticism. He probably wondered why someone would find fault with him. He was only doing his job, but Rue wasn't going to put up with the criticism. One thing was for sure—Jacob Rue was not afraid to resign.

Editor Cook changed his opinion of Rue several years later. Cook wrote, "The raiding of two gambling houses at Long Branch last week was the joint work of the prosecutor and the sheriff. J.B. Rue, the new county detective, did excellent work in connection with the raid. The people of the county will hail the work with gratification."

Monmouth County Prosecutor Henry M. Nevius. *Courtesy Red Bank Library Historic Photograph Collection.*

The year 1904 was one of different directions for Rue, being appointed to three jobs and resigning from two more of them. In May, Red Bank Commissioner Davis appointed Rue as chief of police with authority over four officers in the department. His salary was $500 per year. A few weeks later, Monmouth County Prosecutor Henry M. Nevius appointed Rue as Monmouth County detective. It would be the first time the prosecutor's office would have two full-time detectives. Jacob Rue was the fourth person ever hired as a detective in Monmouth County. For a while, Rue tried doing both jobs but found the demand too great. After serving the town for five weeks as chief, he resigned. Chief Rue's resignation greatly disappointed many of the township's business owners. They urged him to reconsider, to which he agreed. On August 2, Red Bank commissioners reappointed Rue as chief of police, but less than thirty days later, he resigned a second and final time.

A WILD TIME ON THE CORNER

In August, the commissioners asked Chief Rue to put a stop to "corner loafing" and authorized him to use his nightstick on the loafing men if they refused his orders to move along. Rue was intent on following their orders. He said he "was going to put a stop to the loafing on the street corners" and that he "would arrest anyone—rich or poor, white or black—who persisted in keeping up the practice." A man of his word, Chief Rue did just as he said he would.

On a warm summer night in late August 1904, a group of African American men had gathered on the corner of Broad and Front Streets in front of Sherman's Meat Market. Rue came upon the group and ordered them to disperse. When Rue returned, most of the men were gone, but Richard Byran was still there.

Chief Rue asked Byran why he had not moved away with the others. Byran said he had not heard him give any such order. Rue asked him again to move on and keep the corner clear. Byran said no, he wouldn't. Rue told him he must move on or he would move him. Byran refused again. At that, Rue said, "You'd better come along with me," and grabbed Byran by his arm.

Byran resisted, and a scuffle ensued, attracting a large crowd. Chief Rue called out for help and used his nightstick to subdue Bryan. William Giblin came to Rue's assistance, and in the skirmish, Giblin received a stab wound about an inch deep under his left rib. The young man of Herbert Street lost a lot of blood, but he eventually recovered in the hospital. Byran went to jail.

Rue complained that he was not receiving proper support from the officers and that the town needed more men to properly enforce the law. The town commissioners felt four officers were sufficient but told Rue that if he could show them where more officers were necessary they would appoint them. A meeting was scheduled August 30 to resolve this issue, but instead of Chief Rue appearing to plead his case, he sent the commissioners his letter of resignation.

Jake Rue's latest resignation freed him up to join Charley Strong as the first two full-time detectives in the Monmouth County Prosecutor's Office. The first thing Rue did as a county detective was to purchase new rubber tires for his buggy so he could steal up noiselessly upon law offenders. It was obvious that Rue wanted to do well in fighting crime and that he took his new assignment very seriously.

Four Years as County Detective

The rest of 1904 was relatively uneventful for the new detective. Rue went to Eatontown to try to convince Constable James R. Clark to release his prisoner, Edward Soper. Rue wanted to return Soper to his father's custody, but Clark refused. Mr. Soper was a wealthy lumber merchant. His son was considered demented and had given Clark a difficult time in his capture. Clark released his prisoner directly to Mr. Soper only when he appeared in person and paid him for his troubles. Edward Soper had been a freshman at Hamilton College, but his behavior was so erratic that his father sent him to Bloomingdale Insane Asylum in New York.

In 1905, Detective Rue worked on two capital crime cases: the murder of Italian immigrant Frank Rozzo of West Grove and the brutal beating of elderly Mrs. Morris Naftal in her own home in Asbury Park.

THE FRANK ROZZO MURDER

Italian immigrant Frank Rozzo had been unfaithful to his wife and paid for his sin with his life. On June 12, 1905, Rozzo was shot to death in the streets of the Italian community in West Grove, while his wife, Rosa, holding their infant daughter, watched in utter horror. She pled for his life: "Please don't shoot my husband!" Alleged murderer Michael DeLauro escaped.

Rozzo drove a horse-drawn beer wagon for bottler Henry Benvenga. In four years living in America, police had arrested Rozzo for grand larceny and adultery. During his investigation, Detective Rue learned that Rozzo had also shot and killed a man in Italy. Rozzo's death was the result of a family feud.

The spark that ignited the feud came six months earlier when Rozzo, married with children, and Mrs. Louisa DeLauro, also married with children, left town together. When they did not return, their families wondered what happened to them. What happened was that Frank Rozzo and the young, pretty Mrs. Louisa DeLauro deserted their spouses and their children to be with each other. Together as lovers, Frank and Louisa spent a few days cavorting in New York City and then moved back to the area and stayed in an apartment in nearby Belmar. After about two weeks, Mrs. DeLauro returned to her home and children. Her husband, Annelio, had moved out.

Annelio signed a criminal complaint stating that Rozzo stole his wife. Asbury Park Justice of the Peace Roderick S. Cottene issued a warrant for Rozzo, and police arrested him on May 1 on adultery charges. Rozzo's arrest caused bad blood in both extended families, not only with the men but with the women, too. A heated feud broke out between the two clans, with each side blaming the other. The war between the Rozzo family and the DeLauro family peaked with Rozzo's death.

On the night of the murder, Rozzo was driving his beer wagon through the streets of the Italian community. As he drove down Springwood Avenue, he spotted his wife standing in front of Corrino's Bakery. Mrs. Rozzo, holding their baby in her arms, was arguing with Mrs. Joanna DeLauro Scott. The two women were quarreling loudly in Italian. Their argument attracted a growing crowd, including Annelio DeLauro, his brother Michael DeLauro and his uncle, Joseph Scott. As tempers flared, the argument escalated from words to blows. In the heat of the moment, Joseph Scott knocked Mrs. Rozzo to the ground.

Frank Rozzo was in his wagon when he saw Scott hit his wife. He stopped his horse and was ready to spring out to help her, but Michael DeLauro saw Rozzo coming. DeLauro jumped up onto the step of the wagon and fired four shots, wounding Rozzo in the leg. DeLauro then ran down Springwood and turned on Avenue A, with the wounded Rozzo chasing after him. Mrs. Rozzo ran after her wounded husband with her baby in her arms. Annelio DeLauro and Joe Scott soon gave chase, easily passing the hysterical Mrs. Rozzo. Frank Rozzo, with a bullet in his leg, eventually fell to the ground on the corner of Springwood Avenue and Avenue A. Michael DeLauro kept on running and never stopped. As Annelio and Joe approached, Mrs. Rozzo screamed out, "Please don't shoot my husband!" but her words fell on deaf ears. About four steps away from the fallen Rozzo, Scott fired three shots. From about the same distance away, Annelio also fired his revolver into the fallen man. Two of their bullets struck Rozzo, one under his right arm and the other in his abdomen.

Monmouth County Prosecutor Henry M. Nevius assigned Detective Jacob Rue to investigate the case. The Rozzo homicide case was one of Rue's early capital crime case assignments as a county detective. Later that night, Detective Jake Rue and Neptune Police Officer William A. Griffin went to Joseph Scott's house and took him into custody. The DeLauro brothers were nowhere to be found.

The day after the shooting, Rue went back into the Italian community, but no one was talking. Detective Rue believed the DeLauros were hiding nearby. He immediately offered a reward for any information leading to the capture of the alleged murderers. Police circulated a flyer with text written in Italian, "Carente per L'omicido" (Wanted for Murder), with a picture of Michael DeLauro, but no one came forward.

It was good police work by Asbury Park Detective Eddy Hankinson, who developed information that led him to believe the DeLauro brothers were hiding nearby in the woods at Point Pleasant. Hankinson notified the Neptune Police Department. With help from Officer Griffin, the officers went to search the wooded area around the train station.

About 3:00 p.m. Saturday afternoon, Officer Griffin thought he recognized one of the DeLauros hiding in the briars. Griffin fired a shot and thought he inflicted a flesh wound on DeLauro's leg. Officer Griffin gave chase, but DeLauro escaped. The sighting by Griffin confirmed Hankinson's suspicion, so they called for more help. Before darkness fell, a swarm of police officers from neighboring towns had formed a posse and surrounded the area. Detective Rue joined the posse. Griffin took his position hiding behind the flaghouse south of the Bay Head Train Station. Asbury Park Police Chief William B. Steelman searched a house in Point Pleasant three or four times but was unsuccessful in finding either of the DeLauro brothers.

In Hankinson's own words:

> *I gathered a reward from Monmouth County Detective Jake Rue on my information. I took Griffin, colored policeman, and went to Point Pleasant looking for these people. I made a search of the woods near the house which Chief Steelman had searched and put Annelio DeLauro up. The cat briars were so thick that we couldn't get out to get him, but we did get out in time*

Asbury Park Detective T. Edward
Hankinson worked with Rue on
several murder cases. *Courtesy
Hankinson's grandson Donald Voorhees.*

*to see him go in another woods away down the rail road. I phoned Jake Rue
and he came and brought some help with him. We surrounded the woods
and that night about 2:00 o'clock he came out and tried to make a get-away
and we got him.*

By the light of the moon, Officer Griffin saw a man emerge from
the woods and walk on the tracks. Police drew their revolvers and
immediately surrounded him. Exhausted and starving, Annelio DeLauro
surrendered. His brother Michael was nowhere to be found. Detective

Detective Jacob B. Rue Jr. (1873–1933)

Rue and the other officers escorted DeLauro to the jail in Point Pleasant and called an interpreter.

Through the interpreter, Annelio DeLauro told the police that he had been bringing food and clothing to his brother. His wife told him that the police were looking for him, too, so he hid in the woods. Detectives transferred their shackled prisoner to the county jail in Freehold, where the accused murderer would await trial. Annelio DeLauro and his uncle Joseph Scott pleaded not guilty to the first-degree murder of Frank Rozzo and spent the next six months waiting in jail facing the death penalty. Michael DeLauro escaped, never to be seen or heard from again.

The trial of *State of New Jersey v. Annelio DeLauro and Joseph Scott* started January 29, 1906, before the elderly, gray-haired Judge Charles E. Hendrickson in the Monmouth County Courthouse at Freehold. Facing death by hanging, the two prisoners entered the courtroom looking nervous and pale.

Monmouth County Prosecutor Henry M. Nevius presented the state's case. Nevius wanted to prove that although Michael DeLauro had shot first and partially wounded Rozzo, it was the bullets fired at close range by Annelio DeLauro and Joe Scott that had killed Rozzo. The trial was expected to last several days. Prosecutors for the state called seventeen people.

Attorneys for the defense called thirty-one people to testify, including twenty-two eyewitnesses who said that they saw Michael DeLauro shoot Rozzo. All twenty-two witnesses swore they saw the wounded Rozzo chase after Michael DeLauro. They all testified that Rozzo fell to the ground at the corner and DeLauro kept running.

Joseph Scott took the stand in his own defense. In recounting his actions on the night of the murder, Scott said he approached his wife and Mrs. Rozzo when they were quarreling. When it looked like Mrs. Rozzo was going to hit Mrs. Scott, he hit Mrs. Rozzo to prevent his wife from getting hit. Scott said he heard four shots and then saw Rozzo and DeLauro running down the road. Scott's version of the story was that he stayed in front of Corrino's Bakery with his wife. He said he heard a second round of gunshots farther down the road but did not see who fired them.

Annelio DeLauro said he had worked all day at the Point Pleasant Train Station and then returned home and stayed in all evening. He claimed that he was not there when the women quarreled, was not on Avenue A and did not see, hear or do the shooting, and he did not own a revolver.

The trial lasted four days. Detective Rue was not called to testify. After an hour of deliberation, on February 2, 1906, the jury returned a verdict of not guilty for both men on all counts. The fact that Mrs. Rosa Rozzo, along with twenty-two eyewitnesses, implicated only Michael DeLauro in her husband's murder seemed to bear much weight on the jury's decision. Judge Hendrickson ordered the defendants be set free. A large crowd of about fifty Italian men met DeLauro and Scott and escorted them to the nearest saloon to celebrate the jury's decision and their release from jail.

Police never captured Michael DeLauro. He disappeared. It is not known where he went or what name he used in hiding. Although innocent until proven guilty, it seems that alleged murderer Michael DeLauro may have gotten away with the murder of Frank Rozzo.

WILLIAM BROWN INVESTIGATION

In late November 1905, three boys in a rowboat found the body of William Brown floating in the South Shrewsbury River. Brown was the night watchman in Sea Bright, a position he held for fifteen years. He was also the sexton at Sea Bright Methodist Church. The teenagers—James Thorsen, Arthur Benson and Axel Forsman—were out for a row Sunday afternoon when they noticed his body. At first they thought Brown had been robbed and beaten and his body dumped into the river because his pockets were empty, but medical science proved otherwise. Dr. James Reed did an autopsy and discovered that Brown's death was an accident. Dr. Reed said that Brown's cause of death was due to drowning and that he found no evidence of any injuries prior to his body entering the water. Despite Dr. Reed's findings, Prosecutor Henry Nevius assigned Detective Rue to investigate the incident and ordered Coroner John T. Tetley to hold a coroner's inquest.

Rue learned that Brown had been seen drinking heavily in the barroom at John J. Brohm's Grand Central Hotel with Albert Nelson, a Swedish fisherman, the night before he died. Rue concluded that due to the effects of the liquor, Brown accidentally stumbled into the water on his own. He supported the conclusion of Dr. Reed and closed the investigation.

MARY NAFTAL MURDER CASE

Mrs. Mary Naftal was born in 1830 in Germany. She was seventy-five years old, in poor health and alone when she was killed about a week before Christmas in 1905. Her husband Morris was in New York City on business.

Detective Jacob B. Rue Jr. (1873–1933)

Her son Henry was in Philadelphia. The *Asbury Park Press* called it "one of the most dastardly murders ever committed in this state."

Mrs. and Mrs. Naftal lived at 151 Main Street in Asbury Park. Her neighbor, Mrs. G. Goldberg, suspected foul play after noticing that a bottle of milk had been left on the back doorstep for days. Mrs. Goldberg called the police, who went over to the Naftal house and made the horrible discovery. There they found Mrs. Naftal's body underneath a mattress with a handkerchief stuffed in her mouth and her hands and feet tied with window cord. The elderly woman had been smothered to death, and her body had lain there for a week. Intruders had ransacked the Naftal house. They tore apart mattresses and ripped up the carpeting. Her jewelry was missing, and her pocketbooks were empty.

Mrs. Naftal had been frequently seen walking around Asbury Park wearing diamonds thought to be worth thousands. Morris Naftal confirmed as missing a pair of diamond earrings, a diamond crescent pin, two diamond bracelets, one bar diamond pin, one three-stone diamond pin and ten or twelve diamond rings. He placed the value of the stolen jewelry at $7,500 and said that another $1,800 in cash was missing. Mr. Naftal offered a $2,000 reward for the arrest and conviction of his wife's murderers.

Detective Rue got the assignment. Within twenty-four hours of the discovery of the body, Rue arrested Howard F. Morris as an accessory before the fact. Rue questioned Morris to "the third degree," during which Morris made damaging comments about his friend Frank Perdoni. Perdoni ran a fruit market across the street from the Naftal house. Morris's comments to Rue resulted in him finding evidence that led to Perdoni's arrest. At Perdoni's place, detectives found a piece of rope cut from an awning—the same type of rope used to tie Mrs. Naftal's hands. They learned that right after the murder, Perdoni paid off several long-standing bills. When they asked Perdoni to tie a knot in a piece of rope, the knot that he tied was the same knot used on Mrs. Naftal.

Before this all occurred, Morris and Perdoni were longtime friends. At the time of the murder, both men played the ponies and were broke. Morris admitted that they went to rob Mrs. Naftal but not kill her. They used chloroform to subdue her, but the results were accidentally fatal. Morris agreed to be the star witness for the defense at Perdoni's trial. Because of the information received and his agreement to testify, the state dropped all charges against Morris. Perdoni pled not guilty and hired attorneys Charles E. Cook and E.W. Arrowsmith.

At Perdoni's trial, Morris testified that it was Perdoni's idea, and that he said they should join up to rob the home. Detective Rue took the stand and gave testimony for the state. The jury was out just over an hour but came back with a not guilty verdict. Chief Justice William S. Gummere of Newark ordered Perdoni released. The evidence, they said, was only circumstantial.

HENRIETTA JOHNSON MURDER CASE

In 1906, Detective Rue arrested African American Samuel Johnson for first-degree murder. Under the heavy influence of alcohol, Johnson brutally beat his wife Henrietta to death. Rue responded quickly to the call and arrived at the scene in Middletown to find a woman's beaten body lying in a ditch. Rue saw a fence nearby and climbed through a hole in it that led to a field. At first he thought he saw a stump, but as he approached, he realized it was a man crouched over. Detective Rue told the man to stand up, but Johnson refused. Rue pulled out his revolver and convinced Johnson to calm down enough to allow Rue to handcuff his prisoner.

With Johnson locked up in the county jail in Freehold, Monmouth County Prosecutor MacDonald called a coroner's inquest, at which County Detective Rue took the stand and testified. The coroner asked him what he had seen when he got to the scene. Rue said, "I found a body lying on Cooper's Road, on the right-hand side, in a ditch, head down, partially undressed, with a man's trousers on."

"Did you institute a search?"

"I saw an opening in the fence and some tracks going up there, and I walked up, and it was quite a steep grade, and I saw a dark object lying down; it looked more like a stump or log. I went over and found it was this defendant here."

It was "Sam Johnson, apparently asleep or dead, I didn't know which at that time. I took my coat off and hung it on the fence and I went back and found he was alive and turned him over and put the handcuffs on him. I put one on one wrist, and he put up some argument and I used persuasion; and in doing so I noticed his hands were very much swollen, as if he was hitting something very hard."

"Did he resist you?"

"Well, yes, as a drunken man would. I brought him to Red Bank and locked him up. I also warned him at that time in the presence of Mr. Theodore C.E. Blanchard that anything he said would be used against him."

The report of the coroner's inquest stated that "upon the oath of various witnesses, we do find that the said Henrietta Johnson came to her death on the twenty-first day of January, 1906, and that her death was caused by blows inflicted by Samuel Johnson the defendant."

Judge Charles E. Hendrickson sentenced Johnson to twenty years at hard labor in the state prison.

REBECCA TRAYNUM MURDER TRIAL

Rue captured another murderer that year by traveling by rail to Chicago, where he arrested Edward Brown. Brown was wanted for a murder committed two years earlier in Long Branch and was hiding in Chicago using the alias Edgar Smith. Brown pleaded not guilty to murdering his

Detective Eddy Hankinson kept a handwritten diary of the criminals he captured and rewards he earned. *Courtesy Hankinson's grandson Donald Voorhees.*

43

girlfriend, Rebecca Traynum. Rue testified for the state at his trial. On May 21, 1906, the jury in Freehold found Edward Brown guilty of murder in the first degree. Judge Hendrickson sentenced him to death. The New Jersey Legislature had recently enacted a law allowing electrocution as a means of execution, but Monmouth County did not yet have funds available to build an electric chair.

On June 29, the State of New Jersey executed Brown by hanging him from scaffolding in the Monmouth County Jail in Freehold. On the day of the execution, Brown wore a black suit with a black tie and had a black hat pulled over his eyes. Just before he took his place under the dangling rope, he murmured, "God have mercy on my soul." The hanging of Edward Brown in 1906 was the last legal hanging in Monmouth County. Rue did not attend the execution.

Rue continued his work for the Monmouth County Prosecutor's Office in 1907 but would soon move on to a completely different project. Before the year was over, he worked again with Asbury Park Detective T. Eddy Hankinson to arrest four boys from Manasquan for breaking and entering and robbery. During the winter, Edward Johnson, Edward Hedden, Harold Truax and Edward Lane, ranging in ages from eleven to seventeen years old, looted several empty cottages along the beach at Manasquan and sold the plunder to junkmen. The houses were part of the Lockwood Bungalow Colony. After some severe questioning by Detective Rue, the boys admitted to more than a dozen burglaries.

Of a more serious nature that year, Detective Rue investigated four deaths in the county. He also formed the Red Bank Bureau of the New Jersey National Detective Agency in 1907. It elected John Sheehan as president, William J. Doing as secretary and Jacob Rue as chief. Other directors were James Norman, Theodore W. Collier and George Woods.

AYERS CAPTURE

James Ayers started getting in trouble at a young age, getting expelled from Red Bank public grammar school. When he was an employee of James H. Bates of Little Silver, Ayers began forging checks drawn on his employer's account. He signed his boss's name on eleven checks made out to himself for a total of about $200. Rue captured him in New York and returned him to justice in Monmouth County, where Ayers pleaded guilty. On December 8, 1904, Judge John E. Foster sentenced him to three years in New Jersey State Prison.

His mother, Mrs. Sarah Ayers, sent a petition with numerous signatures to New Jersey Governor Edward C. Stokes, which influenced the Board of Pardons. They agreed to release Ayers on parole. After serving one year and four months, Ayers was set free.

After being released on parole, Ayers was soon right back at it in 1907, forging his employer's name and cashing checks for himself. Police notified the local banks and, on May 17, got a call from a teller in the First National Bank of Freehold that Ayers had just cashed another forged check.

Detectives Rue and Elwood Minugh sped out to Freehold. Ayers was already wanted for forging a check in Long Branch. The teller in Freehold told them that Ayers had just left the bank and was playing pool at the Railroad Hotel and that he had been drinking. Rue and Minugh joined with Freehold Constable William D. Hulse and entered the front of the hotel, but Ayers saw them coming and was sober enough to escape quickly out the back door. The officers yelled, "Halt!" but Ayers ignored them. They ran to get Ayers and thus began a wild chase down the busy streets of downtown Freehold. At midday, Ayers ran down Main Street with revolver drawn. He stayed on the sidewalks, where frightened shoppers and millhands saw his

Monmouth County Detective Elwood Minugh worked with Rue on several major cases. *Courtesy Minugh's grandson Ed Sinker.*

gun and took cover. Ayers began shooting as he turned down Throckmorton Street, and the detectives fired back. Ayers was a fast runner, going down McLean Street, then onto Randolph Street, then Institute Street. He was gaining distance on the pursuing officers until Constable Hulse finally jumped into a wagon and cornered him. That gave Rue a chance to catch up, handcuff Ayers and take him to the county jail. Ayers was charged with two counts of forgery, burglary, carrying a concealed weapon and drawing a revolver.

Ayers pleaded guilty a second time. Before pronouncing the sentence, Judge Foster asked Ayers if he had anything to say for himself. Ayers told the judge he had a habit of gambling and when he lost at gambling, he lost his head. That was the only reason Ayers gave for forging the checks. Judge Foster sentenced him to seven years in prison. Ayers took the sentence with a smile, saying that he expected to get twelve years and was surprised he got off so easy.

NICK CATRAMBONE MURDER

It was Thanksgiving night, November 28, 1907. About twenty Italian immigrant men crowded into the poolroom behind Peter Ianicelli's barbershop at 1220 Springwood Avenue. Ianicelli lived above his shop, in the heart of the Italian community in Asbury Park.

The men were drinking and smoking and having a good time. They took turns rolling dice as they stood around the pool table trying their luck. Some were luckier than others. That night, Nick Rozzo's luck wasn't so good. Nicholas Catrambone's luck was worse; in fact, it was deadly. That night in Ianicelli's crowded, smoke-filled poolroom, with twenty Italian men watching, Nick Rozzo shot Nick Catrambone in the face point blank and killed him.

Rozzo had been drinking heavily and was upset about not winning anything all night. He had come to the raffle with his tenant and friend, Jimmy Sinicato. When one of Rozzo's throws was declared a foul, it was the spark that lit the fire. It was a legitimate call; one of the dice rolled up against a man's leg while he was sitting on the pool table. The foul call eliminated any chance Rozzo had of winning, and Rozzo got angry. An argument began to heat up as others joined in. As Ianicelli later described it, "You know how it is with these Italians." Ianicelli saw trouble coming and didn't like what he saw. He tried to calm them down, but no one was listening. "There was a lot of hootin' and hollerin'," Ianicelli said, and he was unable to stop it.

Detective Jacob B. Rue Jr. (1873-1933)

By then the argument had turned into a drunken brawl. Rozzo stood up in the doorway and brazenly declared that he could lick the best man in the crowd and for him to step outside. In a drunken daze, Rozzo drew his revolver from his pocket and fired. Nick Catrambone, standing just a few feet away, fell to the floor with a bullet through his head. He never regained consciousness.

Catrambone, fifty-six years old, was a native of Catanzora, Italy. He had come to New York about four years earlier. He was survived by his wife, Rosa, his son Albert of New York and his daughter Mrs. Ann Ianicelli, wife of Peter.

After the shooting, Rozzo and Sinicato ran out of the house and across some backyards toward Borden Avenue. A few Italians gave chase; some fled the scene; some stayed in the poolroom. Rozzo, on the run, fired wildly, but all his shots landed harmlessly. Rozzo and Sinicato disappeared into the dark of the night.

About 9:00 p.m. that night, Asbury Park Police Officers Clarence Vernon Mooney and Thomas Broderick were standing in front of 1035 Springwood Avenue when they heard the shots. Someone told them it came from the back of Ianicelli's barbershop, where a crowd was beginning to gather. The two officers found Catrambone lying on the floor but still barely alive. He was breathing heavily and choking. He lived only a few minutes more. Officer Mooney searched all the men, found no weapons and started taking the names of the witnesses. They told the officers that Nick Rozzo had shot Catrambone and that Jimmy Sinicato was with him on the run.

Broderick knew Rozzo well from past run-ins. He described Rozzo as about five feet, eight inches tall and 150 pounds, with a flat face and small mustache. Rozzo had stooped shoulders and walked with his feet pointing out. Broderick knew where Rozzo lived with his wife and two children and went to his house on Garfield Avenue. He found the front door unlocked and the bed still warm, but no one was in the house.

From there, Broderick and Mooney went to Joe Scott's house at 1418 Springwood Avenue. There they found Sinicato hiding behind some barrels in the backyard and arrested him. Police brought Sinicato to headquarters, where Detective Rue was waiting. Rue questioned him intensely, but Sinicato wasn't talking. Sinicato had been in the United States only twenty months. He boarded at Rozzo's house, paying $2.50 per month for a room, and worked as a shoveler.

At police headquarters, Detective Rue searched Sinicato and found some revolver cartridges in his pocket. Sinicato said he had found them and picked them up off the street. He claimed he didn't know what they were. Sinicato said he couldn't answer any more questions because he didn't understand English, but when Coroner MacDonald called him a liar in English, Sinicato resented the remark with alacrity. Police searched Rozzo's sister's house and his place of work in Belmar, but Rozzo was nowhere to be found. Police kept a close surveillance on his wife and sister.

Detective Rue was frustrated in his investigation. Nobody was talking. Rue believed that Rozzo was still hiding in the same neighborhood. He felt that Rozzo was somewhere near the scene of the crime in the Italian community and that his friends were helping to conceal his hiding place. Rue had heard that Rozzo was a member of a special society of some sort and that he was assigned to kill Catrambone but that Rozzo had killed the wrong Catrambone. Rue had heard that the intended victim was Ralph Catrambone, nephew of the murdered man. They said Sinicato signaled the hit by hitting Ralph Catrambone in the face. Some believed Rozzo was too drunk to realize he had killed the wrong man.

Coroner MacDonald impaneled a jury and brought them to the morgue to view the body. With assistance from Monmouth County Prosecutor Henry Nevius, MacDonald questioned fifteen witnesses. MacDonald called Peter Ianicelli to testify first. With voice quivering and tears in his eyes, Ianicelli told the jury the story of how his father-in-law was shot that night. Ralph Catrambone, John Lee and Gustav Spino were in the poolroom that night and testified to what they saw. In the end, none of the testimony helped police find Rozzo.

Through an interpreter, Jimmy Sinicato answered questions from Nevius, but he contradicted himself on several occasions. Sinicato's twisted answers angered Nevius to the point where he gave up asking questions and ordered Sinicato held without bail. The jury quickly agreed that Nick Catrambone came to his death by a pistol shot wound at the hands of Nick Rozzo.

This inquest jury also took an unusually bold step by publicly criticizing Asbury Park Police Chief William H. Smith. The jury found that Chief Smith "had been very neglectful in his duties in this case." They claimed that Smith did not give his officers specific instructions to apprehend the suspected killer. They accused Smith of not giving the Long Branch police and other neighboring towns a description of Nick Rozzo and noted that he failed to appear at the coroner's inquest despite being subpoenaed to testify. Smith did not appear in person but sent Constable Lott C. Hubbert as his representative. Nevius blatantly accused Smith of being lax in his endeavors to track down and capture Rozzo.

Adding to this swelling disproval, Prosecutor Nevius made known his disgust when he learned that Chief Smith released Sinicato even after he refused to make any statement. "I suppose if the police had caught the man who committed the crime they would have let him go too." Clearly the prosecutor's antagonistic remark to the press showed how strained the relationship was between himself and Chief Smith.

Despite the criticism, Chief Smith stood his ground. Smith had the backing of Detective Jacob Rue. The next day, Chief Smith called a newspaper reporter to headquarters and gave him his prepared statement. "I do not think it proper for a chief of police to take the public into his confidence in matters of this kind," he began. "To make public the work of the police department is to give warning to the escaped criminal and to his friends who may be secreting him. As to future plans, I have nothing to say." In his defense, Smith said that the day after the murder, he sent one of his officers to Long Branch with a description of Rozzo. He claimed he telephoned Chief James Layton at 8:00 a.m., who confirmed he had met with the officer and had the description.

Chief Smith said he sent four officers to Belmar on a lead and he sent another officer aboard the 11:00 p.m. train to Long Branch to search for Rozzo. The next day, he sent officers on trains to Philadelphia, New York, Jersey City, Lakewood, Farmingdale and Red Bank. His department spent the entire day searching trains and watching passengers who arrived at the depots.

Chief Smith had two hundred circulars printed, written in Italian, giving a description of the alleged murderer and offering a $300 reward. He gave the flyers to Paul Pupilla, the victim's stepson, for distribution. Smith had officers posted watching outgoing steamships leaving the Port of New York; he personally visited and solicited aid from the police departments of Jersey City, Hoboken, Brooklyn and New York City. Smith added, "This watch of the outgoing steamers is still being maintained and at a great expense to the city."

Smith confirmed that Detective Rue was supportive of his work. He said on the night of the murder, Detective Rue came down in an automobile and had been back a second time. In reviewing his steps, he said that Rue "has gone over the case with me and he approved of my course." Rue told Smith that he felt "everything was being done to apprehend the murderer."

In conclusion, Chief Smith said, "I have given you a pretty good idea I think, of what we have been doing, though I have not told you all, because as you know, the case is not settled and the publicity would not help the case but rather aid the escaped murderer." From Chief Smith's statements, it appears that he was doing the best he could and that Prosecutor Nevius was misinformed of the chief's efforts.

About three weeks after the Catrambone funeral, a report surfaced that the elusive Nick Rozzo was still in town. Rumors were flying that Rozzo was having trouble raising enough cash to pay for his fare back to Italy. Ralph Catrambone told police that someone who knew Rozzo told him that he saw Rozzo walking past the poolroom dressed as a woman. A black veil partially hid his face, but not enough to avoid masking his identity. The man wore a black skirt, a shirtwaist and a woman's hat. As soon as Rozzo realized he had been recognized, he turned and ran down the street, jumped a picket fence and disappeared among the shacks. Police never saw or heard from Rozzo again.

Rue in the Private Sector

On December 14, 1907, Rue resigned from the Monmouth County Prosecutor's Office. He had spent almost four years on the job as a county detective. During that time, the prosecutor assigned Rue to several prominent cases. He was commended for his clever detective work, important arrests and obtaining full confessions. Rue ended his first term as a Monmouth County detective because he did not want his official duties to suffer while he occupied his time with his new project. He wanted to be able to give his full attention to his newly purchased properties.

Rue's wise decision and timely purchases proved insightful. In 1908, Henry Ford produced the Model T, the country's first affordable car. As these cars started to appear on the streets of Red Bank, so did the need for a repair shop. Rue's transition from horses to cars, and from detective work to automobile garage owner, was a successful attempt to keep up with the times.

RUE'S AUTO GARAGE AND BOAT WORKS

Rue was now free to devote his entire attention to his new automobile garage and boat works business on Front Street. In November, he purchased Joseph A. Throckmorton's lumberyard and John Abbott Worthley's adjoining coal yard. He paid $11,000 for the lumberyard. These two prime properties in downtown Red Bank gave Rue three hundred feet of frontage on the

A NEW PLANT

UNDER CONSTRUCTION

✳ ✳ ✳

Automobiles!
Yachts!

✳ ✳ ✳

J. B. RUE,

West Front Street,

RED BANK, N. J.

Above: Rue's Auto Garage and Yacht Works in Red Bank. *Courtesy Rue family.*

Left: Rue's advertisement for "A New Plant." Red Bank Register, *November 27, 1907.*

Shrewsbury River. Rue tore down the old buildings and removed the coal shutes and trestles. Less than a year after his purchases, the Red Bank town commissioners approved Front Street to be paved with bricks.

For auto repairs, Rue built a two-story, 51-foot by 128-foot garage. He purchased the newest lathes and ironworking and woodworking machines available for the separate machine shop. For the boat works, Rue built new docks and had the river dredged to form a 130-foot by 190-foot basin allowing access during high and low tide. He built a large 50-foot by 120-foot shed for winter boat storage and railways connecting the shed and dock. He installed a one-thousand-gallon main gasoline tank with a pump that measured outflow so boaters would know how much gas they received. Finally, he added a salesroom to sell the newest models of gasoline engines.

In all, Rue spent over $50,000 on improvements. He said he wanted to make it the very best that was possible to have. His business was the largest auto and boat facility in Monmouth County. On April 29, 1908, Rue said his plant would be in good running order within two weeks. Improvements would continue to be made, and new machines would be constantly installed. On May 13, 1908, he ran a full-page advertisement in the *Red Bank Register*.

One of his first orders came from Colonel Edward W. West of Trenton. Colonel West asked Rue to build him a forty-five-foot speed launch powered by a 150-horsepower Simplex engine.

Bad luck struck on Saturday afternoon, June 27, 1908, when a spectacular fire damaged Rue's docks, pumps, tanks and boats. Rue's employee, James Chadwick, forgot to screw on the vent cap of the main fuel tank, which at the time held about seven hundred gallons. Without being vented, gasoline overflowed down to the docks and onto the surface of the Shrewsbury River. Gasoline saturated the sawdust and bark filling of the dock.

Not noticing the spillover, Charles Bennett lit a cigar and threw the match overboard. Bennett, in charge of the power launch *Wanderer*, was sitting on the boat talking with William Hamilton. Instantly, as the match hit the gasoline on the water, a huge flame arose and a large black cloud of smoke billowed up. The stern of the *Wanderer* caught on fire. Bennett jumped overboard to escape and swam safely to shore. Hamilton was flung several feet by the explosion of the sudden flame. Someone rang the alarm, and the firemen arrived quickly. They tried using two streams of water and chemical powder extinguishers, but neither seemed to have any effect on dousing the gasoline-on-water flames. The firemen could only use the streams to contain the burning area. Five hours later, the gasoline had finally burned itself

J. B. RUE'S
AUTO GARAGE
=AND=
LAUNCH WORKS.
Open Night and Day.
TELEPHONE 285.

Full Line of Supplies for Automobiles and Marine Engines.

All Repairs Completed at Time Agreed On.
Expert Mechanics in All Branches.
Tire Repairing and Battery Charging a Specialty.

We are prepared to duplicate any part of an Automobile, Launch or Marine Engine.
The Launch Works are in charge of Douglas Riddle of Oceanport, one of the most expert boat draughtsmen and boat builders in this part of the state.
The Garage Shop is in charge of William Kubeck of New York City, who was formerly and up to May 1st, foreman of one of the largest repair shops and garages in New York City. Mr. Kubeck brought three of his assistants with him.
With the facilities and machinery in this shop, all repair work, of whatever character, can be turned out very quickly. The machinery for cutting gears and doing similar work is especially complete, and includes all the latest improved machines for this purpose.
We will make a specialty of caring for launches, rowboats, etc., at a moderate sum per week or by the season. This branch is in charge of Captain Walter Chadwick, formerly captain of the Constellation, who will have charge of the dock and gasolene station, and who will be on duty day and night.
Prices in every department will be reasonable and work will be guaranteed. With all our latest improved machinery we are able to turn out work about 25 per cent less than has been charged heretofore in this locality.

28-32 West Front Street,
RED BANK, N. J.

Advertisement for J.B. Rue's Auto Garage. Red Bank Register, *May 13, 1908.*

out. Rue estimated that he lost several hundred gallons of gas. The tank, a brand-new automatic pump and the dock were destroyed.

After the fire, Rue hired George Varney of White Plains, New York, to rebuild his new buildings and had them constructed of reinforced concrete. Rue's Red Bank Garage was the first building in Red Bank to be completely constructed of this fireproof material.

In 1910, Rue leased his boat works to Frederick Rumpf Jr. and leased his docks to George and Forman Matthews. He sold his *Anna T III*, a thirty-nine-foot wooden boat with a gasoline-powered engine, to Andrew White.

ANNOUNCEMENT.

The Fireproof Garage

at 30-32 West Front Street, known as "RUE'S GARAGE" is now under new management.

M. R. VAN KEUREN & SONS took charge on July 3d.

A new, full stock of the best Tires, Lubricating Oils, and all Automobile Sundries will be kept in stock. Vulcanizing of Tires and Shoes and all kinds of repairing done by EXPERT WORKMEN.

CHARGING OF BATTERIES AND STORAGE OF CARS.

Standard Oil Co.'s Best High Test **GASOLINE.**

CHARGES REASONABLE.

The Red Bank Garage.

Announcement for "The Fireproof Garage." Red Bank Register, *July 14, 1909.*

White renamed the boat *Olivia B.* and planned to use it to haul sand from Highlands to Red Bank for making cement blocks. Rue sued Mrs. E.C. Hazard for nonpayment for repairs he did to her automobile, and the judge ruled in his favor for $250 in damages and costs.

RED BANK THEATER

Venturing into another new arena, Rue bought the Frick Lyceum from Fred Frick, one of his boating customers. Rue purchased the two-acre property with 132 feet of river frontage in October 1910. Frick had bought the property about the same time as Rue bought his boat works and had built the theater with a capacity of fourteen hundred seats.

Rue completely remodeled the theater and its surrounds. He built a plank boardwalk from Front Street to the theater entrance for pedestrian access. To make it easier and safer for theatergoers on foot, he limited people in carriages and autos access only through the separate entrance on Wharf Street.

Rue hired crews to repaint the interior light green and red. He redecorated the proscenium arch, overhauled the heating system and rearranged the seating for better views of the stage. He refurbished the women's sitting room and added a men's smoking room. He hired a maid for the women's

RED BANK THEATER

FORMERLY FRICK LYCEUM

⟜FORMAL OPENING⟞

MONDAY EVENING, OCTOBER 24

Alfred E. Aarons and Louis F. Werba Present

HARRY KELLY

In the Most Recent of all Musical Comedy Successes   A Sequel to "His Honor the Mayor"

DIRECT FROM THE NEW YORK THEATER

"THE DEACON AND THE LADY"

Presented by a Metropolitan Company of Seventy-Five People, Including a Chorus of Fifty

AUGMENTED ORCHESTRA

CLARA PALMER, MAYME C. EHRUE, MADELYN MARSHALL, DOROTHY HOMER,
E. D. WYNN,   FLETCHER NORTON,   W. W. BLACK,   PERCY JENNINGS.

The Same Identical Cast, the Same Beauty Chorus, the Same Magnificent Scenic Equipment
as Presented on Broadway at the New York Theater

Seats on Sale at Cooper's Drug Store, Saturday Morning.   Prices $1.50, $1.00, 75c., 50c.; Boxes $2.00.

Rue opened his Red Bank Theater with this advertisement. Red Bank Register, *October 19, 1910.*

room and employed a large force of ushers. The stage and dressing rooms were improved. He renamed the building the Red Bank Theater and raised prices of admission. Box seats went for two dollars each.

The formal reopening, held October 24, 1910, featured the short-lived two-act musical Broadway comedy *The Deacon and the Lady*, starring Harry Kelly as a country deacon. The show was produced and directed by Alfred E. Aaron and Louis F. Webra and was set in Floodville, Vermont, and New York City. Originally titled *Deacon Flood* and renamed, the show was planned as a sequel to *His Honor the Mayor*. It had a seventy-five-member cast, an augmented orchestra and fifty-member choir. *The Deacon* also debuted actor Ed Wynn as "Jupiter Slick." Main characters included Clara Palmer, Mayme Gehrue, Madelyn Marshall, Fletcher Norton and William Black. At his newly refurbished Red Bank Theater, Rue also booked billiard exhibition matches and skating contests.

Detective Jacob B. Rue Jr. (1873–1933)

RARITAN VIGILANCE SOCIETY

In 1911, the Raritan Vigilance Society was organized when horse thieves were active in rural areas of Monmouth County. Over the previous few months, a dramatic increase in robberies had taken place. Members joined the society for protection against thieves. Members George A. Holmes and James C. Hendrickson of Middletown, James Byram of Red Bank, Joseph Sproul of Hazlet and George Titus of Belmar had all been robbed. All reported barns being broken into and losses of horses, buggies, wagons, harnesses, blankets and other equipment.

The Raritan Vigilance Society was associated with the Raritan Grange. Society members elected Aaron Morris president, James C. Hendrickson vice-president, Charles X. Crawford treasurer and J.C. Brower secretary. At a meeting that May, members voted to accept Jake

Monmouth County Prosecutor John S. Applegate Jr. *U.S. passport photo.*

Rue as a member. At the same time, Prosecutor John S. Applegate Jr. hired Rue to investigate the recent robberies and gave him authority to make arrests. Rue listened to the society's victims' stories and followed up a number of clues. Based on his past county detective experience with horse thieves, Rue determined the robbers were operating out of Long Branch.

HORSE THIEVES ARRESTED

$50 Reward.

A reward of Fifty Dollars is offered for the arrest and conviction of the person or persons who took the following goods from J. P. Sproul's barn at Keyport on the night of Sunday, October 20th.

A silk plush lap robe, one side green, reverse side black.

Also a tan, white and blue plaid blanket,————

Also the following articles from the barn of Frank P. Sproul the same night.

One plush lap robe, brown one side, black on the reverse.

One whip.

The reward is offered by the

Raritan Vigilance Committee,

J. T. BROWER,

Secretary.

Rue posted this fifty-dollar reward as part of the Raritan Vigilance Society. Red Bank Register, *October 23, 1912.*

Rue suspected Long Branch painter Jacob Spivock and assigned his assistant to keep Spivock under surveillance. Spivock had previous run-ins with the law and was unaware that he was being watched. Rue's assistant observed Spivock drop off a buggy at Frank C. Bedle's place in Keyport and learned that he would return to pick it up the next day. When Spivock returned, he tied the buggy to the back of his wagon and began heading back to Long Branch. Rue had alerted Joe Sproul to be on the road to watch as he passed, which he did with his son. They identified the buggy in tow without question as the one recently stolen from their barn and held Spivock until Rue came and arrested him. Spivock told Rue that he had bought the buggy from Joseph Waldman.

On May 21, Rue and Red Bank Constable Elwood Minugh went to Long Branch and arrested blacksmith Joseph Waldman at his home. Upon learning that Waldman had bought the buggy from painter Jacob Rosenberg, they went to Rosenberg's house and arrested him too. Rue searched Rosenberg's house and found a stolen blanket belonging to Sproul and a set of burglary tools. All three thieves—Spivock, Waldman and Rosenberg—were Russian Jewish immigrants of Long Branch. Spivock pleaded not guilty on two counts of breaking and entering and was found not guilty. Rosenberg pleaded guilty to grand larceny. Rue testified for the state at his trial. Judge John E. Foster sentenced him to three years in state prison for each burglary, including the ones at Sproul's, Titus's and Hendrickson's farms, for a total sentence of nine years behind bars. After three years, Rosenberg was released on parole.

MONMOUTH COUNTY FAIR

The Fifth Annual Monmouth County Agricultural Fair was a huge success. On August 30, 1912, Rue was Governor Woodrow Wilson's personal escort. During the horse show, Rue showed off his riding skills. While performing one stunt on a well-trained horse, Rue's cap fell off. He galloped across the field at full force and then suddenly stopped short just before reaching the fence, thus avoiding jumping over or colliding into the fence. His antics

Rue was Governor Woodrow Wilson's personal escort at the Monmouth County Fair, August 30, 1912. Wilson is standing in the car; Rue is to the right looking up at him, behind Detective Minugh with the large mustache. Nine weeks later, Wilson won the presidency in a landslide. *Courtesy Red Bank Library Historic Photograph Collection.*

amused the crowd. Sensing that he had the crowd with him, Rue turned around and picked up his hat while riding his horse at full speed. A reporter wrote that "Mr. Rue's doings created almost as much attention as the events of the horse show."

Governor Wilson was campaigning for the presidency. He spoke to the crowd about urging more use of schools and churches as community centers. Many cheered his speech. Besides the horse show, there were contests for largest produce, livestock, cutest babies, a steer show and schoolchildren's exhibits.

J.B. Rue Detective Agency

Rue returned to his investigative activities, this time as head of his own private detective firm, in December 1916. He rented office space in the Second National Bank Building in Red Bank and advertised that he and his assistants were ready and able to do residential and commercial investigations. Rue hired Vernon Bennett to work with him. Bennett worked as a Red Bank patrolman. He had passed the exam for county detective, but the prosecutor's office did not hire him because of his slight build. Together, Rue and Bennett made several arrests, but Rue's Detective Agency only lasted a few years.

J. B. Rue Detective Agency.
Formerly chief of detectives, prosecutor's office. Residential and commercial contract investigations. Suite 7, Second national bank building, Red Bank.—Advertisement.

Rue ventured into the private sector, advertising his detective agency in Red Bank. Red Bank Register, *December 13, 1916.*

POISONED PEN CASE

As a team, Rue and Bennett secured evidence using marked postage stamps to arrest Miss Mary Purtell for sending poisoned pen letters to her former neighbor. Over a four-year period, Mrs. Eva Bewsick of Rumson Road had received disturbing poisoned pen letters. The letters were handwritten and signed only by "One Who Knows." They accused Mrs. Bewsick's husband of having improper conduct with a relative of Purtell. Mr. Bewsick was a local factory manager. Mary Purtell was the daughter of Andrew Purtell, a well-known New York politician and hotelier. Mrs. Bewsick and Mary Purtell were neighbors in Little Silver before the Bewsick family moved. Both women were members of the Little Silver Sewing Club until a disagreement occurred and Mrs. Bewsick resigned. The letters usually arrived a few days after Mrs. Bewsick held a party at her house, and the tone of the letters became increasingly hostile, with strongly worded messages. One letter contained a newspaper clipping of a woman who had received poisoned pen letters and had shot another woman. The letters were spiteful and of a malicious character. Their intent was to cause trouble in her family. Mrs. Bewsick called it maddening.

Frightened about the escalating, threatening tone of the letters, Mrs. Bewsick went to the authorities. She asked Monmouth County Prosecutor Charles Sexton to find and stop the sender, but Sexton's investigation ended without discovery. Finally, Mrs. Bewsick hired Rue's Detective Agency, and they got results. She brought the letters to Rue and explained the situation. Rue suspected Purtell and put her under surveillance. She was seen mailing a letter just before Mrs. Bewsick received another threatening letter. Rue got a warrant for her arrest and asked Constable William W. Wilson to arrest Mary Purtell of Riverside Avenue for sending the poisoned pen letters. She was arraigned before Judge Edward W. Wise and held on $500 bail. Purtell insisted that she was innocent and called the charges ridiculous. She said that her sister Eva Purtell was also receiving similar letters.

The case came before the grand jury on October 3, 1917, but the grand jury failed to find an indictment against Mary Purtell. Despite Rue's surveillance and marked postage stamps, experts compared the handwriting in the letters to samples of Mary Purtell's handwriting and said they did not even remotely resemble each other.

Caiazzo and Woolley Murder Investigations

MAFIA HIT CAMILLO CAIAZZO

By 1920, Rue had secured his second appointment as a detective to the Monmouth County Prosecutor's Office. For the next five years, Detective Rue was busy solving crimes and arresting villains throughout the county. In 1921, Rue paid for a newspaper ad offering a fifty-dollar reward for the recovery of William Peterson's stolen motorcycle. He traveled to Boston and arrested Clarence Hendrickson for atrocious assault and battery on his wife, and he arrested James Ayers for a third time. Rue also worked on several big murder cases, including the Mafia ordered hit on Camillo Caiazzo in Belmar, the unsolved murder of fisherman John Woolley in Spring Lake and the murder of Salvatore Santaniello in Little Silver.

On a hot sunny afternoon during the summer of 1921, four young men set out in a rowboat to catch some delicious blue claw crabs. They headed to Tuckers Cove on Shark River, a local hot spot for catching crabs down at the Jersey Shore. Instead of coming back with a bushel of blue claws, Isaac Sorrell, Charlie Bennett, Louney Cousins and John Gant came back with a dead body in tow. It was August 8, 1921. Sorrell spotted the body first, lying on the bottom of the cove in shallow water, about two hundred feet from the shore.

The body was weighted down with two large stones weighing about twenty-five pounds each and tied with clothesline rope, one around his knees and the other tied around his neck. The dead man was dressed in

A firm believer in offering reward money for information, Rue placed this newspaper ad. Red Bank Register, *November 23, 1921.*

black mohair pants, a striped silk shirt and an expensive pair of black shoes. He wore a gold ring with a green emerald stone and gold cuff links. He looked to be about twenty-five years old, maybe Italian, with a smooth face and short, dark hair. No one recognized him. They called the police. All he had in his pockets were a one-dollar bill and a heavily faded, washed-out envelope that looked like it was addressed to "_____ Caizzo, 44_ ___ Twelfth Street, New York City."

Police removed the corpse to Hardy's Undertaking Establishment in Belmar, where Monmouth County Detectives Jacob Rue, Jack Smith and Charles Davenport viewed the body. The detectives forwarded the information from the soggy letter to the Bureau of Missing Persons in New York City. A day later, the bureau confirmed that Camillo Caiazzo of 445 East Twelfth Street was missing. They notified Caiazzo's brother-in-law, Joseph Babonno, who went to Belmar to identify the body.

Babonno told the detectives that Caiazzo lived with his mother. He had only been in America about fourteen months and spoke very little English. He had gone to Belmar to buy a business, and when he left the house he had about $600 in his pocket. While Babonno talked to the police, Detective Rue investigated the scene of the crime.

Rue discovered the spot on the shore where the rocks used to weigh down the body were taken. The rocks came from the Riverview House on Shark River, owned by Salvatore Rose. The clothesline used on the body was also similar to that found on Rose's property. Rue took Rose into custody but was reluctant to talk to reporters about his findings.

Rue placed him under arrest as a material witness, and Rose was held without bail.

Rue questioned Rose, which led to the arrest of Bartolo Fontanna. Under intense questioning, Fontanna confessed to killing Caiazzo and also to fifteen other murders by a gang known as the Good Killers. Rue worked with the Italian squad of the New York Police Department in rounding up several other members of this group.

Fontanna said he was ordered, under force of death, to lure Caiazzo to Shark River and kill him. He told Caiazzo that he could help him find a business. When he arrived, Caiazzo saw Rose's shotgun and wanted to try bird hunting. They went into the woods, where Fontanna used the gun to shoot him and then "bury" the body in Shark River.

Rue testified for the prosecution at Rose's trial before Judge Samuel Kalisch on March 23, 1922, in Freehold, but after three days' deliberation, the jury found Rose not guilty. Fontanna retracted his plea of not guilty, and Judge Kalisch sentenced him to life imprisonment with hard labor.

Fisherman Woolley

Less than three weeks later, on August 25, 1921, John Woolley, owner of a fishing pound in Bradley Beach, was found dead in his home on the corner of Madison and Third Avenues in Spring Lake. A single bullet punctured his chest. His wife, Annie, was visiting her sister in Elizabeth, New Jersey. His son, Alvah, was at the movies in Asbury Park with a friend.

Pound fishing along the Jersey Shore was a dangerous and difficult way to make a living. Each morning at dawn, Woolley's six-man crew would row out past the breakers in heavy, thirty-foot-long wooden surfboats. These boats were designed with low freeboard to make hauling heavily laden nets in over the side easier. In rough surf, waves could easily swamp the long boats. Chances of surviving a difficult swim in frigid water nearly a mile off shore were not good. Sometimes, overnight catches would trap large schools of weakfish or tuna feeding near the shore. The day's haul would weigh over a ton. From the full boats ashore, the men loaded the fish into baskets onto horse-drawn carts to the packing plant. There they packed their catch in ice and shipped it to market.

Woolley's crew once caught two four-hundred-pound porpoises in his pound, which he sent to the New York Aquarium in Brooklyn. Wrapped in burlap, the two porpoises arrived within four hours of their capture.

Above, left: Fisherman John Woolley of Spring Lake, murder victim. *Courtesy John A. and Virginia Woolley.*

Above, right: Mrs. Annie Woolley, widow. *Courtesy John A. and Virginia Woolley.*

Left: Woolley's son Alvah was at a movie with a friend the night his father died. *Courtesy John A. and Virginia Woolley.*

Detective Jacob B. Rue Jr. (1873–1933)

Woolley's pound boats at Bradley Beach. *Courtesy John A. and Virginia Woolley.*

A good day's catch of tuna at Woolley's processing plant in Bradley Beach. *Courtesy John A. and Virginia Woolley.*

Superintendent Leonard B. Spencer named them Flip and Flop, but in captivity they only lived for ten days. During that time, the mammals were the center of attraction in the great round center tank.

On the night of the murder, Alvah came home and found his father dead on the floor. Alvah called Dr. William W. Trout and the police. Monmouth County Prosecutor Charles Sexton assigned three detectives: Jack Smith,

Dr. William W. Trout of Spring Lake, Woolley's family doctor. *History of Monmouth County, New Jersey, Lewis Historical Publishing Co., 1922.*

Schindler Detective Agency. *Courtesy John A. and Virginia Woolley.*

Charles Davenport and Jacob Rue. Alvah hired Raymond Schindler of Schindler Investigations, a private detective agency from New York City. During his investigation, Detective Rue must have done something to impress Schindler. In his final report, Schindler wrote that "County Detective Rue, from the standpoint of competency, in my opinion, is better than his other two associates."

Rue arrived at the scene about 4:00 a.m. that morning and began making observations. With Smith and Davenport, he took fingerprints from the stairway wall. The weapon used to shoot Woolley was missing. Outside, they found scrapings on a first-floor windowsill that seemed to indicate a forced entry, but Woolley had died with two rolls of money in his pockets.

Rue told Schindler that "the county finding is that of suicide." Rue based this decision on the direction of the shot and the deceased's previous attempts at suicide. Rue theorized that Woolley came home that night, disgusted because his girlfriend and former employee, Maria Hurley, was going with another man, and went to his room and killed himself. When Alvah arrived and discovered what had happened, he hid the gun to keep the disgrace from the public. Rue claimed that the gun found in the son's possession was examined by an expert who found powder in one chamber. Alvah told police he was at the movies in Asbury Park with a friend at the time of the shooting. The name of Alvah's friend and the name of the movie they saw went unreported. Schindler also did not report whether Alvah admitted to removing the murder weapon.

Alvah Woolley hired Private Detective Raymond Schindler of New York City to investigate his father's death. *U.S. passport photo.*

Schindler disagreed with Rue's suicide theory.

It does not appear to me that such is the case. The position of the body, the conditions which preceded the shooting and the good humor of the deceased does not in any way indicate suicide. It does not seem probable that the deceased would enter his home, have something to eat, go to a spare room which he was not in the habit of entering, not remove any of his clothes, not even his hat and kill himself. He was a man that understood the handling of firearms and was in dread of suffering. He would not shoot himself in the shoulder to commit suicide. Knowing what he did about guns he would not likely put his thumb on the trigger to shoot himself in the head, and this is the only way he could have held the gun to get the shot on the angle in which it entered.

Schindler concluded that John Woolley's death was not a suicide by his own hand but that he was murdered by person unknown.

So who killed fisherman John Woolley? Was it Woolley himself or a burglar who got scared off? Could it have been his son, Alvah, or Maria Hurley's jealous brother Walter, a gambler and a fighter who was nowhere to be found at the time? We'll never know. The murder, or suicide, of John Woolley remains an unsolved case.

Ayers Captured a Third Time

On Monday night, July 24, 1922, James Ayers and Fred Slater robbed the U.S. Post Office in Little Silver. They stole about $200 of merchandise, mostly belonging to Postmaster Clark P. Kemp. They gained access by prying loose a sill under the rear door, which allowed enough room to reach up and dislodge the bar that held the door locked.

Ayers took about six hundred cigars and several cases of high-priced cigarettes, leaving the low-quality ones behind. He took a typewriter, fountain pen, a dollar's worth of pennies and all the letters to be delivered, but he left behind the insured parcels. He left the safe untouched but later said he planned on returning to blow it up. Ayers took his loot and hid in a nearby abandoned house.

Word of the heist spread quickly around Little Silver. People in town immediately suspected "Ginger" Ayers, as locals had named him for his fiery red hair. Recently paroled from state prison, Ayers had been seen hanging around the post office.

The next day, Jim Corbett brought Robert Cook over to look at his vacant house with hopes of selling it. Upstairs, the bedroom door would not open. They pushed hard, and before the door suddenly closed back on them, they saw a pistol and letters lying about. Corbett and Cook ran out of the house, told the neighbors to keep their eye on it and called Detective Rue and the Red Bank Police.

Detective Rue arrived quickly and found the front door unlocked. As he pushed, shots began to fly from inside. One bullet penetrated the door

Rue's double action Colt 45 revolver, with chip missing on grip. *Photo by George Joynson.*

and struck Rue in his right hand. The single shot shattered bones in his last two fingers and took a chunk off the handle of Rue's double action Colt 45 revolver where he was gripping it. Rue left the scene to see a doctor, but not for long. A serious bullet wound wasn't going to stop Rue from doing his job. He hurried back to the house where the desperate criminal, surrounded and willing to shoot, was taking refuge. By then, a slew of police officers and detectives, armed neighbors, firemen, soldiers from Camp Vail with bright spotlights and spectators surrounded the house. Police Officer William Mustoe of Red Bank was part of the mass of officials. Upon his return, Rue took charge of the posse and ordered everyone with a gun to start shooting at the house. The barrage lasted more than an hour. By now, it was after midnight.

They shot out the glass in every window and riddled the clapboard sides with bullets but encountered no return gunfire. With Rue leading the way, several officers cautiously approached. They entered the house with revolvers drawn, shooting through each door and closet before entering. They searched the first and second floors but did not find Ayers.

"He isn't in there. I guess he has got away, unless he is in the cellar," Rue said. With that, the firemen turned on their hoses and began to flood the cellar with water. Part of the foundation caved in from the heavy streams. When the water reached about five feet deep, Ayers unexpectedly came out, emerging from the cellar near the collapsed wall. With his hands held high in the air, gasping for breath and fear in his eyes, Ayers surrendered. The mob cried, "String him up!" but police took him to jail.

The next day, a reporter from the *Red Bank Register* wrote,

> *Throughout the siege, Mr. Rue showed the utmost daring and coolness. He stood in front of the house most of the time and was a shining target if Ayers had wanted to shoot him…Ayers had fastened the front door after he shot Mr. Rue and he could have picked off a number of his attackers with ease.*

Doctors said that Rue might lose two fingers due to the bullet wound. The bullet shattered bones in his last two fingers, and doctors thought they might have to be amputated. If not, they might stiffen, become useless and interfere with Rue's capabilities as a detective. "If this proves to be the case, I am going to have the fingers taken off," Rue said. After all these years of fighting crime, a bullet wound in the hand, nearly getting shot to death and losing two fingers was not going to stop Jacob Rue.

Rue said he was surprised that Ayers was still in the house after they had searched it. He said he really thought "his bird had flown" because the water in the cellar was so deep, no one would have been able to survive in it. It was the third time Detective Rue arrested the career criminal James "Ginger" Ayers.

About noon on Sunday, July 30, Ayers broke out of the county jail in Freehold. Workers had removed the wooden roof during the remodeling job going on at the jail and had replaced the roofing with thin metal sheets. As was the usual practice, guards let the prisoners out of their cells to get their meals. Three prisoners—Ayers, Stanley Kaminski (charged with murder) and Joseph Lewis (serving time for disorderly conduct)—climbed to the top of the building, pushed the metal sheets aside and then climbed down the roofer's scaffolding and scrambled away. Warden Edward Cashion only found out about the escape about an hour later, when some local citizens reported three suspicious men walking toward Monument Park. Once again, officers, soldiers, farmers and firemen formed a posse to track down the escaped prisoners. Detective Rue rushed to Little Silver, only to find out that it was a false lead.

Early the next morning, William Hawkins, a farmer of Robbinsville, saw fresh footprints and heard his dog barking. He spotted two men in his corn field and called the New Jersey State Trooper Patrol Station in Freehold.

Trooper Sjostrom with his Harley Davidson motorcycle, circa 1928. *Courtesy New Jersey State Police Museum.*

He reached Captain Eric P. Sjostrom, who hopped on his Harley Davidson motorcycle and sped out to Hawkins's farm. Trooper Sjostrom approached the exhausted and hungry prisoners and, with gun drawn, told them to surrender. Ayers and Kaminski immediately put their hands up without resistance. Trooper Sjostrom ordered the men into the back of Hawkins's truck and drove them back to Freehold.

Once fed, showered and back in his cell, Ayers talked up a storm. He told the warden they had been walking toward the Matawan Train Station but took the wrong road and ended up at Gordons Corner in Marlboro. Ayers told them they dumped Lewis along the way because he didn't have much endurance and couldn't run fast.

On August 3, 1922, Ayers was convicted of atrocious assault and battery with attempt to kill, of breaking and entering and of carrying a concealed weapon. Judge Rulif V. Lawrence sentenced him to fourteen to twenty years. Ayers threatened, once he got out, to kill Judge Lawrence, Detective Rue and Court Officer Bernard Seltman. Lawrence also ordered Monmouth

Detective Jacob B. Rue Jr. (1873–1933)

Captain Eric Sjostrom was a member of the first class of New Jersey State Troopers in 1921. *Courtesy New Jersey State Police Museum.*

County Prosecutor Charles F. Sexton to further indict Ayers on a felony charge of escaping from jail and on federal charges of stealing mail from the U.S. Post Office. Guards took the forty-year-old career criminal back to the New Jersey State Prison in Trenton to begin serving his fourth prison term. Despite getting shot in the hand and Ayers's death threats, Detective Rue stayed on the job.

Bootlegger Salvatore Santaniello

O n the morning of January 25, 1923, local painter Patrick Bates drove to work on the house owned by Winfield S. Wainwright. Wainwright was a lumber merchant who lived on Silverside Avenue in the Little Silver section of Shrewsbury Township. On his way, Bates spotted a body lying on the side of Seven Bridges Road near Little Silver Point. The body was in full view of passing traffic, propped up on an embankment. Bates went on to Wainwright's house, where they called the Red Bank Police Department. Since the area was outside Red Bank jurisdiction, they called the Monmouth County Prosecutor's Office. Prosecutor Charles Sexton assigned Detectives Jacob B. Rue and Jack Smith to the case. Upon receiving the call, Detective Rue dropped everything and sped to the scene of the crime. He was the first officer to arrive. Rue did not recognize the man but learned the next day that Bates had discovered the body of Salvatore Santaniello, a wealthy Italian immigrant bootlegger from New York City.

Rue searched the man's pockets and found about ten dollars, a gold watch and chain, a ring and a scarf pin. Having these items, Rue ruled out robbery. He also found a small account book written in Italian showing numerous sale amounts and addresses. One sale was for $2,556. On some weeks, Santaniello netted more than $5,000. Rue started to think that the murder was the result of a bootlegger's vendetta. During the Prohibition Era, bootleggers often quarreled over territory disputes. Rue also found on the body a return train ticket to New York City and a blurred check for $1,070 dated January 10, 1923. The check was endorsed by John Calandriello, a

Winfield S. Wainwright
of Little Silver reported
the Santaniello murder.
*Courtesy Wainwright's
granddaughter Anne
Wainwright Jordan Sellers.*

bottler from Fair Haven. At the site there were fresh automobile tire tracks leading to Fair Haven. Rue kept the clues to himself and told reporters only that he expected to make an arrest in a few days.

Two days later, Rue gave up on solving the Santaniello murder case and publicly voiced his frustration. He told a newspaper reporter from the *Asbury Park Press* that the Santaniello case "may be placed forever among the unsolved mysteries of the county."

Rue was grossly upset with the actions of his co-worker, Detective Charles O. Davenport. Angrily, Rue told reporters, "The murderers in this case probably will never be found, due to the inefficiency of Detective Charles O. Davenport." Rue accused Davenport of divulging sensitive information about the case to reporter Beverly W. Brown, who promptly had her story published in the *Red Bank Standard*. Rue did not want the information about the check leaked to the public. He thought the details of the check could have been used to find the killer and bring him to justice.

Detective Jacob B. Rue Jr. (1873–1933)

Ocean Township Police Chief Frank Eisele, on his Harley, investigated the unsolved Herry murder case with Rue. *Courtesy Ocean Township Police Department.*

Detective Davenport downplayed Rue's harsh comments and his charge of being inefficient. Davenport said he had no reply other than that "Mr. Rue is apt to say most anything."

For whatever reason, Rue had come to the right conclusion. To this day, the names of Salvatore Santaniello's killers are unknown to all but those who did it. As Rue predicted, the Santaniello case remains among the unsolved murder mysteries of Monmouth County.

RUE NEARS THE END

Due to his poor health, Rue decided to retire. He submitted his resignation to the Monmouth County Prosecutor's Office on December 12, 1926. He turned in his county-owned automobile but kept his revolver. William Mustoe, a ten-year veteran of the Red Bank Police Department, filled his vacancy. As

Rue in retirement, teaching his young grandson Jacob B. Rue IV to smoke a cigarette. *Courtesy Rue family.*

Rue's replacement, Mustoe embarked on a career as a Monmouth County detective that lasted thirty-six years. Rue retired and spent the next eight years living out his life near his family.

Jacob Bergen Rue Jr. died of a massive heart attack on December 3, 1933. He died in his own home at 43 West Front Street, where he had lived most of his life. He had suffered previously from milder heart attacks. Rue named his wife, Anna, as executrix of his Last Will and Testament, and his remains are buried in Old Presbyterian Churchyard in Shrewsbury, New Jersey.

Section Two

Detective William S. Mustoe (1890-1981)

Mustoe's Early Years

I am a firm believer in the brotherhood of mankind.

William Stanley Mustoe was born February 7, 1890, in Brooklyn, New York, the youngest of six children born to English immigrant parents. William was nine years old when his father died. Soon after, his mother, Florence, remarried.

At the turn of the century, young William was living with his mother and stepfather, Arthur Moore, an English immigrant and musician by trade. Growing up on Hewes Street in Brooklyn with five older siblings and a stepfather might not have been too easy back then. As a teenager, he ran away from home. One day, he made the decision to go and never looked back. Mustoe hopped aboard a freight train and got off at the station in Red Bank, New Jersey.

William Mustoe was just eighteen years old when he first got his name in the local newspaper. On July 15, 1908, Red Bank Police Officer Horatio Shutts arrested him and his co-worker, Peter Klippel, for cutting tree branches on Broad Street. Mustoe and Klippel worked for the Shore Electric Company and were clearing the wires. The trees were in front of Dr. Biddle Garrison's house. Mrs. Nellie Garrison gave the boys permission to cut the branches, but the trees belonged to the township. Under the new ordinance, the penalty was a maximum twenty-dollar fine. Court Recorder Edward W. Wise decided to issue no fine since it was their first offense but instead issued them a warning.

William Mustoe married Anna Sanborn on September 7, 1910, and the next year, their daughter Thelma was born. A few months after the birth of

Dr. Biddle H. Garrison, Red Bank surgeon. *Courtesy Red Bank Library Historic Photograph Collection.*

Dr. Jeremiah Sayre, the "country doctor" with an office in downtown Red Bank. *Courtesy Red Bank Library Historic Photograph Collection.*

their only child, Mustoe fell off a high ladder and was injured. He worked as an electrician for the Public Service Lighting Company and was repairing a streetlight. Co-worker William Decker saw Mustoe going over and tried to steady the ladder, but the force was too much. The ladder slipped, and Mustoe fell onto the brick-paved street below. The fall knocked him unconscious. He broke his jawbone, knocked some teeth out and broke his arm in three places. Dr. Jeremiah Sayre reset the bones. Mustoe took some time off from work and fully recovered.

During 1913–15, Mustoe was a chorus member of Troop B, Red Bank Cavalry of the New Jersey National Guard. He served as a private during the Mexican border trouble and was rated a fine marksman before receiving an honorable discharge.

TEN YEARS AS RED BANK POLICE OFFICER

In February 1916, Mustoe took the civil service test to become a policeman. People considered his application a "dark horse," since he did not file until the last minute. He was the only candidate not acquainted with Mayor George M. Sandt and two councilmen who administered the oral, written and physical tests. Mustoe must have had good answers when Mayor Sandt asked him to explain the duties of an officer and what he would do under certain emergencies. He passed all parts of the tests successfully, and his score was the highest of the five men tested. It was the first time that the Red Bank commissioners used the civil service exam to select applicants to the police force. Mustoe got the job with a starting salary of seventy dollars per month. His first night on the job was March 2. At that time, Officer Mustoe was five feet, eight inches tall and weighed 183 pounds. He had brown hair, brown eyes and a ruddy complexion.

In March 1921, Officer Mustoe caught Fred J. Pettit and Howard Lamberson in the act of robbing Millford F. Tetley's store in Red Bank. Tetley was a public notary and keeper of deeds. Lamberson had a wife and child, and Pettit was his younger brother-in-law. Early in his career, Mustoe developed the skill of getting confessions from offenders. Under Mustoe's questioning, Pettit and Lamberson confessed to robbing several other stores in the area. They told Mustoe they were unemployed, unable to find work and desperate for cash. Lamberson and Pettit admitted to a three-month-long robbery spree, starting with the Economy Grocery Store that January. The two thieves told Mustoe that they found their first heist so easy they

Red Bank Mayor George M. Sandt hired Mustoe as a police officer in 1916. *Courtesy Red Bank Library Historic Photograph Collection.*

decided to continue. They broke into Joseph N. Hance's office and then the Red Bank Junior High School building. They robbed the A&P Grocery Store, the Sugar Bowl Candy Store and Myron Brown's office, all within a few blocks of one another in Red Bank.

Justice of the Peace Edward Wise ordered Pettit and Lamberson locked up in the county jail without bail to await action of the grand jury. The judge ordered that they be committed to the New Jersey State Reformatory. The township commissioners cited Officer Mustoe's work on this case as an outstanding achievement. Mustoe was quickly establishing himself as a trusted civil servant.

In July 1925, Mustoe was reelected president of the Red Bank Police Benevolent Association. The association held events such as an annual ball in St. James High School auditorium to raise money for its sick and death benefits fund.

Escaped Leopard

On June 23, 1926, Monmouth County Prosecutor John J. Quinn Jr. offered Officer William Mustoe an appointment to the prosecutor's office as a county detective, to fill the vacancy left by Jacob Rue's retirement. Mustoe accepted the promotion and resigned from the Red Bank Police Department. Township officials honored Mustoe's achievements as a police officer with a dinner feast. Detective Mustoe's first day on his new job was July 1, 1926. It was the start of a long and illustrious career as a county detective that lasted thirty-six years.

One of his earliest and most unusual cases as a county detective was that of an escaped leopard. In August 1926, Mustoe visited the Twin Brook Zoo in Middletown to investigate rumors of a leopard hunt. He interviewed zoo owner Oliver W. Holton.

Editor J. Mabel Brown of the *Matawan Journal* wrote that Holton had created a hoax to use as advertising. The editor accused Holton of making the story up as a publicity stunt. Hoax or no hoax, the publicity created interest, and people were visiting the zoo in droves. Holton showed Mustoe the freight bill, the animal's empty cage and leopard tracks in a nearby field.

Mustoe reported to Red Bank Police Chief Harry Clayton that the story of an escaped leopard was no hoax. Mustoe described it as a serious situation and noted that precautions should be taken. Based on Mustoe's observations, Chief Clayton told reporters, "I am thoroughly convinced that the leopard escaped and is roaming the fields. I want to warn the people of

Twin Brook Zoo owner Oliver William Holton, of Catasauqua, Pennsylvania. *U.S. passport photo.*

Front and back leopard tracks. *Courtesy Jerome Philippe.*

this neighborhood to remain on their guard." Mustoe believed it was no hoax, and so the hunt began.

Holton had paid $400 to purchase the large cat from Henry Bartell of New York. Bartell hired Ricardo Malguthor, who had accompanied the animal from Singapore. Malguthor said the large cat had been in captivity about three months and was vicious. Once it arrived in New York, Bartell shipped it by truck to Twin Brook Zoo. The spotted leopard arrived at the zoo in Middletown on August 6, and that night it somehow slipped out of its cage. It was about five feet in length, stood three feet tall and weighed about ninety pounds. Fearing the worst scenario with his escaped leopard on the loose, Holton quickly offered a $100 reward for it, dead or alive.

As you can imagine, an escaped leopard in rural Monmouth County in the 1920s was big news and caused general hysteria. Big-city newspaper reporters came pouring into town and stayed for a week. Big game hunters came to Monmouth County in droves, ready to shoot to kill. One hunter claimed to be an expert on leopard behavior, having killed twenty-eight leopards. Frantic mothers kept their children inside the house. Farmers counted their chickens and goats on a daily basis. Calls to police regarding leopard sightings flooded Middletown and other neighboring towns' police headquarters.

Expert animal trainer John P. Snyder didn't help to calm the fears. When a reporter asked his opinion, Snyder replied, "That leopard is mean. He hates human beings and I am surprised that he has not killed someone out there." Snyder said the escaped leopard would not attack horses but that its hunting habits would make it particularly dangerous to humans. "It will spring from behind," he said. "Men might be looking for it and it would be crouched down in the tall grass right beside them. It would not stir until they had passed and then would leap from behind. Leopards are quick as lightning."

Detective Mustoe said the prosecutor's office was ready to loan hunting dogs and armed men. Calls claiming leopard sightings came in from places as far as one hundred miles away. Robert Campbell of Nut Swamp said he saw the leopard grab one of his roosters and eat it. Campbell's call drew six carloads of hunters who scoured his farm and fields without finding a trace. Every time Holton got a call of a leopard sighting, he would visit the area to confirm or deny the tracks. After many faulty sightings, New Jersey State Troopers began to have suspicions.

Trooper George Tighe said the people who reported seeing leopard tracks couldn't tell the difference from deer tracks. Some pranksters in search

Left: New Jersey State
Trooper George Tighe
warned the public of the
seriousness of the escaped
leopard situation but
is shown here "goofing
around." *Courtesy New Jersey
State Police Museum.*

Below: Farmer Henry
Eigenrauch of Chapel Hill
got reimbursed for one
hundred chickens killed by
the leopard. Shown here
with his son Herbert in
front of the windmill on
his chicken farm. *Courtesy
Eigenrauch family.*

parties would shoot off their guns just for the excitement. This kind of wild behavior alarmed Tighe. He warned everyone to be cautious. He said that the local county farmers were already more frightened by harm from the excited men in the search parties than of the escaped jungle cat.

Two months later, Willard F. Irons shot and killed the beast in Island Heights, a good forty-five miles to the south of Twin Brook Zoo. His mother had a poultry farm, and she had noticed over the last two weeks that her fowl had been mysteriously disappearing. Willard had heard about the escaped leopard and was suspicious. He set four muskrat traps and one otter trap along the path where they saw the strange animal tracks.

Early the next morning, Mrs. Elizabeth Irons went out to see what her dogs were barking at and came face to face with the spotted leopard caught in the otter trap. She screamed when the leopard leaped, but the chain around its front paw held the angry cat back, shy of its mark. Willard came running and realized that with one or two more leaps, the snarling cat might free itself. He came back with his double-barrel shotgun and shot the leopard.

Handler Ricardo Malguthor displays the dead leopard at Twin Brook Zoo. © *Kathy Dorn Severini, Dorn's Classic Images. Used by Permission.*

Willard and his mother loaded the dead leopard into their car, drove to the Twin Brook Zoo in Middletown and collected the $100 reward. Holton paid Mrs. Irons for eleven fowl that his leopard had killed. He also paid Henry Eigenrauch of Chapel Hill for his loss of one hundred chickens.

Holton put the leopard carcass on display, and as the news broke, many people came to see the dead leopard at the zoo. With the escaped leopard case closed, Mustoe went on to investigate crimes, collect information and arrest criminals. Twin Brook Zoo had trouble with other animals escaping and lasted in business only a few more years.

Captures, Confessions and Kidnappings

TOMLIN CAPTURE

In November 1926, Mustoe recaptured Clarence Tomlin, a twenty-seven-year-old African American inmate from Newark who, for the third time, had escaped from the county jail in Freehold. Authorities had charged Tomlin with six counts of highway robbery. Because of his repeated attempts to flee, Tomlin was being held in solitary confinement.

This was Tomlin's third jail break. In July, he escaped for three days. His second break occurred August 17, when he and William Voorhees made a big enough hole in a sheet-iron wall at the back of their cell to squeeze out and crawl away. They broke through a locked door and exited through the basement.

His third and final attempt occurred October 27, when Tomlin asked jailer Frederick Knight permission to go to the washroom. On the way, Tomlin overpowered Knight. The men wrestled; Knight got two teeth knocked out. Tomlin stole Knight's set of jail keys and let himself out. He then stole a car and drove to New York City.

Detective Mustoe investigated the case. Somehow, he obtained a letter that Tomlin had written to an unnamed person in Red Bank. The letter had the address of where Tomlin was staying in New York City. Mustoe went to the city and quietly confirmed that Tomlin was living at that address. Instead of arresting Tomlin in New York, Mustoe returned to Red Bank and devised a plan to lure Tomlin back so that he could capture him in town. Mustoe's intention was to avoid the delay and red tape involved in the extradition process from New York to New Jersey.

Mustoe sent Tomlin a phony letter inviting him to Red Bank, enticing him with a big robbery job and lots of easy cash. Mustoe cleverly wrote the letter using jail slang and asked Tomlin to help, and he said that afterward they would beat it to the South with barrels of money. Tomlin fell for it hook, line and sinker.

On November 3, Tomlin arrived on the 8:56 p.m. train at the Red Bank Train Station, wearing dark glasses and a handkerchief over his mouth so as not to be recognized. Sergeant Joseph Bray met Tomlin with his gun drawn. Mustoe jumped out from his hiding place and handcuffed him. They brought Tomlin to the Red Bank jail and then took him back to the county jail in Freehold.

Authorities were taking no chances on November 17 in court before Judge Jacob Steinbach Jr. Officers escorted the shackled Tomlin in with one arm handcuffed to Mustoe. Guards were posted at all court entrances. The jury found Tomlin guilty on all six counts of highway robbery. Judge Steinbach sentenced him to forty-four to fifty-six years of hard labor in state prison.

With Tomlin safely locked up at the state prison in Trenton, Detective Mustoe worked on two more murder cases. In 1927, he investigated the sixteen-year-old Rosina Stoble murder in Red Bank, and in 1928 he worked on the Max Turnow murder in Keansburg. Christina Stoble shot her daughter and went to jail. Turnow was fooling around with a married gypsy woman. For an in-depth look at these two cases, see *Murders in Monmouth: Capital Crimes from the Jersey Shore's Past*, by George Joynson, published in 2007 by The History Press, Charleston, South Carolina.

WHITNEY CONFESSION

In January 1929, Mustoe solved another murder mystery by obtaining a confession from fourteen-year-old murderer Belle Whitney. Whitney was an African American unwed mother. She lived with John and Theresa Mackey on Peach Street in Shrewsbury and was Mrs. Mackey's niece.

Belle Whitney and John Mackey attempted to kill Mrs. Theresa Mackey. They tied her hands and hit her with an axe, and she went unconscious. To make it look like an accident, they dragged her to the railroad tracks and left her. The two thought she was dead, but Mrs. Mackey cleverly feigned her death. After they left, she wriggled loose, rolled off the tracks and ran for her life. She ran toward Eatontown, where Officer Harry W. Kirkgarde helped her. Theresa Mackey, bloody from a fractured skull, muddy from being dragged and consumed by fear, told Officer Kirkgarde her story and survived. Kirkgarde alerted the surrounding police, but it was too late to capture Whitney and Mackey.

Thinking that they had just committed murder, Whitney and Mackey fled. With six dollars in their pockets, they took a taxi to Matawan and then a train to New York. Their plan was to hide from authorities by staying on the move. For two days, they rode the subways until their money ran out. Then things got worse.

On the run with no money, the two began to argue. Not realizing Mrs. Mackey had survived, Belle threatened to turn John in for murdering his wife; John threatened to turn Belle in for her part in the murder. They found an empty apartment on Thirty-second Street and decided to rob the adjoining building, which housed a mail-order business. Despite a watchman patrolling the building, the two culprits managed to get to the seventeenth floor but found no food and no money. While Mackey turned to listen for the watchman's footsteps, Belle entirely lost it. In desperation, the young teenage girl hit John Mackey over the head with an iron pipe and killed him. She whacked him three more times, left his body on the fire escape and exited the building onto the streets of New York City.

Whitney went up to a police officer and gave her name as "Bessie Jones" from Boston. She told the officer that she was visiting with her father but got separated from him on the subways. The officer had no reason to doubt her story. He brought the juvenile girl to the Society to Prevent Cruelty to Children, where she was fed and clothed. She told them she had a sister in North Carolina. Soon after that, police officers found Mackey's dead body and were unable to identify him. Since Belle's "missing father" report had occurred about the same time, they asked her to identify the body and she did, continuing with the lie that Mackey was her father.

Back in Monmouth County, Detective Mustoe was investigating the attempted murder of Theresa Mackey. Theresa told Mustoe about Belle's sister in North Carolina. Through the grapevine of intelligence gathering, Mustoe heard about the New York City incident and thought there might be a connection between "Bessie Jones" and Belle Whitney. He hopped aboard the next train into the city and met with Miss Bessie Jones.

Mustoe interviewed Whitney to try to determine her involvement with the attempted murder of Mrs. Mackey. At the time of her interview, Whitney was unaware that Mrs. Mackey had survived. Whitney claimed to be Bessie

Jones from Boston, but Mustoe suspected her alias. Upon further questioning, Whitney broke down and confessed to both crimes. Case after case and with each opportunity, Mustoe was developing a knack for getting confessions.

By now, residents had grown accustomed to seeing stories about Mustoe getting confessions. An article in the *Matawan Journal* read, "The net of the law gathered another victim into its meshes Friday night, when, after a six-hour grilling by County Detective William S. Mustoe, night watchman Charles Woolley, forty-eight-years-old, of Long Branch broke down and confessed the robbery of the Tide Water Oil Distribution plant in Eatontown on Monday last week."

UNDER PROSECUTOR TUMEN

On April 9, 1930, Prosecutor Jonas Tumen asked all the detectives, including Detective Mustoe, to resign so he could appoint his own staff. Mustoe refused, as did the others. Tumen made some harsh changes right from the start, giving his newly appointed assistants private offices but only shared desk space to the detectives who wouldn't resign. He instituted strict reporting for their time on a daily basis. Mustoe endured Tumen's reign and stayed on the job under seven different prosecutors.

That same year, Mustoe worked on the unsolved Salvatore Oriente murder in Asbury Park. Oriente was an Italian immigrant bootlegger who was gunned down while driving his slick Auburn coach. Oriente was conscious at the hospital but refused to say who did it. He was one villain whom Mustoe could not persuade to tell all.

LINDBERGH KIDNAPPING

Detective Mustoe also participated in investigating the 1932 Lindbergh baby kidnapping. On March 1, Charles Lindbergh and Anne Morrow's twenty-month-old son, Charles, was kidnapped from their home in Hopewell, New Jersey. The body of the Lindbergh baby was found four miles away with a skull fracture. Bruno Hauptmann proclaimed his innocence but was found guilty of the kidnapping and electrocuted. Anne's sister Elizabeth, said to have been attracted to Charles, was notably quiet during the investigation and trial.

WANTED

INFORMATION AS TO THE
WHEREABOUTS OF

CHAS. A. LINDBERGH, Jr.

OF HOPEWELL, N. J.

SON OF COL. CHAS. A. LINDBERGH

World-Famous Aviator

This child was kidnaped from his home
in Hopewell, N. J., between 8 and 10 p. m.
on Tuesday, March 1, 1932.

DESCRIPTION:

Age, 20 months	Hair, blond, curly
Weight, 27 to 30 lbs.	Eyes, dark blue
Height, 29 inches	Complexion, light

Deep dimple in center of chin
Dressed in one-piece coverall night suit

ADDRESS ALL COMMUNICATIONS TO
COL. H. N. SCHWARZKOPF, TRENTON, N. J., or
COL. CHAS. A. LINDBERGH, HOPEWELL, N. J.

ALL COMMUNICATIONS WILL BE TREATED IN CONFIDENCE

March 11, 1932

COL. H. NORMAN SCHWARZKOPF
Supt. New Jersey State Police, Trenton, N. J.

Charles Augustus Lindbergh Jr. *Courtesy www.fbi.gov.*

Anne Morrow
Lindbergh. *Missouri
History Museum, St.
Louis.*

On March 8, Mustoe drove to Bedford, Pennsylvania, on instructions from Chief Harry B. Crook on a search to investigate a tip from an unnamed Monmouth County resident. Crook said that his investigation was based on information obtained before the actual kidnapping had occurred. The tipster wanted to remain anonymous but told Chief Crook that if his lead proved true, he would come forward to reveal his identify and testify at the trial.

Mustoe returned from Bedford and stated his conclusion: "Having seen Anne Morrow just prior to the birth of the kidnapped baby, and her appearance then positively indicated that she was about to become a mother. This positively explodes any theory that Elizabeth Morrow was actually the mother of this child." Mustoe cleared up just one loose-ended rumor in a murder and investigation that had many bizarre twists.

Four years later, Governor Harold G. Hoffman decided to reopen the case to conduct his own unofficial investigation. Hoffman trusted Mustoe and requested his services. On January 28, 1936, Prosecutor Thomas R. Bazley agreed to assign Detective Mustoe as a special investigator to the staff of Governor Hoffman. Mustoe spent three months on the Lindbergh case, reexamining evidence and reinterviewing principals. Mustoe interviewed Hauptman's defense attorney, Lloyd Fisher, and defense witnesses William Bolmer and Henry Uhlig. He also reinterviewed General Herbert N. Schwarzkopf. Finally, Prosecutor Bazley asked for Mustoe's return to help with the workload in Monmouth County. On March 5, Bazley wrote Governor Hoffman: "I have a murder case with ramifications in Delaware, a second murder case in Middletown, and a third homicide in Belmar with ramifications in three states." He asked, "I reluctantly write to inquire, in a spirit of cooperation I hope you will never question, whether at this time, you can advise me when you will no longer need the services of Mr. Mustoe."

Hoffman went on to conduct one of the most corrupt governorships of New Jersey. Often referred to as the "Crime of the Century," the notorious Lindbergh kidnapping case still fascinates many people today with alternative theories of what really happened back then. When he retired, Mustoe looked back on working the Lindbergh kidnapping case as "one of the outstanding experiences of my life."

MUSTOE ADVANCES

Toward the end of 1934, an investigation into the Monmouth County Prosecutor's Office found incidences of improper behavior that warranted the prosecutor's impeachment. Prosecutor Jonas Tumen and Chief Crook were severely criticized in the Naughright Investigation for their misconduct in office. The report accused Tumen of gross negligence and misdemeanor of office. Justice Joseph B. Perskie removed Prosecutor Tumen from office and appointed Special Prosecutor Edward Currie to take his place for the remainder of Tumen's term. Tumen was the first prosecutor ever to be removed from office in Monmouth for misconduct.

The first thing Currie did was to suspend Chief Crook. The Naughright Investigation Report had severely criticized Crook's failure to account for money found in confiscated slot machines. Prosecutor Currie promoted Mustoe to chief of detectives, the highest rank a detective could achieve. When reporters pressed him for a statement, Mustoe said, "I will exert myself to the utmost to show Mr. Currie that his confidence in me is not misplaced." Chief Mustoe filled the vacancy until ex-Chief Crook's term expired that April.

Upon accepting the promotion, Mustoe said, "We are public servants and intend to act as such. We intend to assist every police department in the county which may require our help and I want them to know that they can call on us at any time." As chief, Mustoe headed a staff of four detectives: Amerigo Sacco and Leonard Shields of Freehold and Merritt Bristol Kent and Harry Zuckerman of Long Branch.

CAPTAIN MUSTOE

Ten years later, in February 1945, Prosecutor John J. Quinn promoted Detective Amerigo Sacco to chief of detectives and Mustoe to captain of detectives. Sacco's salary was $4,000 yearly. The Board of Freeholders would decide on Mustoe's pay.

Mustoe used his cleverness to catch a thief at Elliot's Pavilion in Sea Bright. In September 1946, managers had complained to him that thieves were looting the bathhouses. Captain Mustoe decided to rig a series of mirrors so he could monitor an aisle along the row of entrances to the bathhouses. Once the mirrors were in position, Mustoe hid in one of the houses and began his watch. His mirrors worked. Mustoe watched a sixteen-year-old boy come out of a bathhouse red-handed with five dollars in his hand. The unnamed boy from Rumson confessed that he had taken it from a woman's purse. He also confessed to previously taking thirty to forty dollars in cash, four watches and a cigarette lighter. His older brother also confessed to taking a watch from one of the bathhouses.

The two boys appeared before Referee John L. Montgomery at Freehold. Montgomery suspended sending the brothers to the State Home for Boys at Jamesburg, and placed them both on three years' probation in custody of their mother.

In August 1952, Captain Mustoe arrested Mrs. Ann Serra Johnston for murdering her ex-husband. Johnston was recently divorced from Malcolm K.F. Johnston, an Irish immigrant and senior law student at Temple University. Ending a long argument over custody of their twenty-month-old son Daniel, she allegedly fired five shots from a .38-caliber Cobra Colt pistol into him. The argument occurred in her apartment at 435 Spring Street in Little Silver. Johnston pled no defense to manslaughter and was sentenced to seven to ten years. Authorities released her on parole after serving three years behind bars.

Detective William S. Mustoe (1890–1981)

Detective William S. Mustoe, endorsed by the executive committee of the Brotherhood of the Presbyterian Church. Red Bank Register, *February 8, 1940.*

During his career as a county detective, Mustoe had created a reputation for being humane in his treatment of law offenders. He said, "I am a firm believer in the brotherhood of man and in every case, I put myself in the other fellow's position before I really get going." He was called "the Cop with a Hundred Hats," and "the Best Dressed Detective" because he was commonly seen wearing different hats on different occasions. A confessed convict once referred to him as "the Man Who Could Make a Horse Talk." Others referred to Mustoe as "the Parson" for his regular service attendance at First Presbyterian Church and his active involvement with the Presbyterian Brotherhood. A well-liked and popular man, Detective Mustoe was even given credit for his ability to pick out the tastiest turkeys for the Brotherhood's Annual Feast.

During his thirty-six years working as a Monmouth County detective, Mustoe came under six different prosecutors. When John J. Quinn, born May 15, 1893, in Red Bank, was sworn in on April 4, 1925, he was the youngest person ever to be appointed prosecutor in New Jersey. Prosecutor Quinn served two five-year terms, from 1925 to 1930 and later from 1940 to 1945. Quinn selected Mustoe for his first appointment to the office.

In 1930, Jonas H. Tumen replaced Quinn until he was removed from office in January 1935. Tumen was the first prosecutor to be removed from office for corruption. Edward William Currie was appointed as special prosecutor,

Prosecutor John J. Quinn Jr. *U.S. passport photo.*

serving just three months to finish Tumen's remaining term. Currie later got elected mayor of Matawan Township.

Following Currie was Thomas Raymond Bazley, who served from 1935 to 1940. Bazley and his young wife, Catharine, enjoyed travel to the Bahamas, Portugal, Bermuda, Cuba, Argentina and beyond during his tenure.

John Victor Carton served two consecutive five-year terms, from 1945 to 1955. Born in Asbury Park, Carton came from a family of lawyers and graduated from Georgetown University and Columbia Law School. Vincent P. Keuper followed Carton and served for seventeen years, from 1955 to 1972. Keuper prosecuted the 1966 sensational murder case of anesthesiologist Carl Coppolino, accused of murdering his wife. Coppolino hired F. Lee Bailey for defense. The jury found him not guilty, ending Keuper's impressive string of thirty-nine consecutive convictions as county prosecutor. "I can't really quarrel with the jury's verdict," he said.

William Mustoe retired one day after his seventy-second birthday, on February 8, 1962. His thirty-six-year-long career is one of the longest any detective has ever worked for the Monmouth County Prosecutor's Office. A month later, Red Bank Mayor George A. Gray held a testimonial dinner in Mustoe's honor. More than one hundred law enforcement officials attended the dinner at Colts Neck Inn, where they presented him with a wallet and cash gifts. The Board of Chosen Freeholders approved his yearly pension of $3,830. Prosecutor Keuper named Detective Merritt B. Kent to replace Mustoe as captain.

William Stanley Mustoe died January 7, 1981, in Pompano Beach, Florida, and is buried in Fair View Cemetery in Middletown, New Jersey. Mustoe was a former leader of Boy Scout Troop 23 in Red Bank and a member of the International Order of Odd Fellows (IOOF), Red Bank Elks and Red Bank Masonic Lodge.

Section Three

Detective Harry B. Crook Sr. (1891-1973)

Gangsters in a Turf War

Harry Bernard Crook Sr. was born in New York City on October 20, 1891, to parents John and Catharine Crook. His father was a carpenter from Scotland. Harry was the first of eight children and grew up in Manhattan. In 1911, he married Anna T. Harvey. He spent seven years in the Seventy-first Regiment of the New York National Guard and, by 1917, had reached the rank of sergeant.

By 1920, Crook was working as an insurance agent living in Irvington, New Jersey, with Anna and their three sons. His physical description was that he was five feet, seven inches tall, weighed 180 pounds and had blue eyes, brown hair and a ruddy complexion. Sadly, Anna suffered from manic depression and committed suicide by shooting herself with a .38-caliber revolver on January 27, 1929.

A year later, Crook and his sons moved to Asbury Park, where he found a job working as a store detective for Steinbach's. At the time, Steinbach's advertised as the world's largest department store. Crook's younger brother Frederick lived with him and worked as a private investigator. On April 1, 1930, Monmouth County Prosecutor Jonas Tumen appointed Harry Crook as chief investigator in the office of the prosecutor. One of Crook's first job assignments was working along with Detective Mustoe, who had seven years in the department. Together, they arrested seven men allegedly running a numbers racket in Red Bank. With Crook in charge, Detectives Mustoe and Sacco raided Stephen Morici's house on Shrewsbury Avenue. Crook had information that Morici was believed to be the leader of the illegal operation.

Left: Chief Crook as he appeared on the front page of the January 3, 1935 *Asbury Park Press* as Prosecutor Currie removed him from office. *Courtesy Crook family.*

Below: Steinbachs—World's Largest Department Store. *Courtesy Library of Congress.*

At the raid, they found six men gambling in his cellar. Crook arrested all of them on charges of lottery and brought them to the county jail. That same year, Crook's first big murder case was that of Italian immigrant bootlegger Salvatore Oriente in Asbury Park.

ORIENTE HIT

On the night of April 16, 1930, Salvatore Oriente was shot through the back of his head while driving his car near the intersection of Bangs and Dewitt Avenues in Asbury Park. Oriente's murder was big news in Asbury Park. Headlines in the *Asbury Park Press* stretched across the top of the entire front page in big bold letters.

Arthur Grayson, who lived across the street from where Oriente's car crashed, heard the shots and called police. "I was getting ready for bed," Grayson said, "when I heard two reports. At first I thought a couple of tires blew out and looking out the window I saw a machine on the sidewalk against the fence of the Bangs Avenue School. I then telephoned police."

Salvatore Oriente was born February 13, 1886, in Quindici, Italy, and had come to America in 1906. The fertile Quindici Valley was ideal for growing good grapes and olives. Oriente left that behind in coming to America. For a while, he worked for the New York and Long Branch Railroad. In 1930, he was still unmarried and lived alone in Long Branch, working odd jobs. He was of medium height, medium weight and brown eyes and black hair.

Oriente was a known bootlegger. During the Prohibition Era, selling illegal liquor was a profitable but risky business. Bootleggers would claim local territories for themselves, and any rival caught selling on their turf was

Asbury Park Press, *April 17, 1930.*

dealt with harshly. Oriente had recently been released from jail after serving a short sentence for a conviction of illegal sale and possession of liquor. Now back on the streets, he may have been trying to reclaim his turf.

Police quickly suspected Salvatore "Chippie" Vivancio of Neptune, one of Oriente's rival bootleggers. Police also learned that several hours before the shooting, Oriente had attended a meeting of bootleggers in a house at 117 Borden Avenue. Word on the street was that the purpose of the meeting was to form a peace pact among rivals, but police theorized that Oriente disagreed with the terms. As Oriente left the house, police believed that one of his rivals from that meeting followed him and shot him.

Grayson's call to headquarters came in at 10:20 p.m. Asbury Park Police Captain Ernest Williams and Sergeant J. Arnold Reed were the first officers to arrive at the scene. They found Oriente slumped over the wheel of his dark blue, low-slung Auburn coach. It appeared that Oriente had lost control of the car as he tried to turn the corner. His car jumped the curb and stopped as it smashed into the school fence. He had a bullet embedded in his head but was still conscious. Captain Williams brought Oriente to Dr. Daniel F. Featherstone's office, who ordered the victim be taken to the hospital.

Williams accompanied the wounded man to Monmouth Memorial Hospital in Long Branch, where the restless Oriente was admitted at 11:15 p.m. Dr. John E. Maher, who recognized Oriente from previous visits, gave his patient some opiates to calm him. He shook Oriente's shoulder and asked if he knew him. "Yes, I do," Oriente replied, but he refused to say anything else. The next day, Dr. Maher told reporters, "Several relatives came to see him while I was there. One of them said he was a brother (although Oriente had no brother) and, after conversing in Italian for a few minutes, left. Another relative came and I refused him admittance because of the patient's serious condition."

Oriente lingered in and out of consciousness for about five hours. During his last hours, Oriente refused to tell Detective Mustoe who had shot him. Sticking strongly to the criminal code of justice, Oriente would not, even on his deathbed, reveal the name of his slayer.

At the crime scene, Captain Williams found large amounts of broken glass, which he thought came from a broken window in the assailant's automobile. He was convinced that Oriente had fired back at his assailant. "From the amount of broken glass at the scene, I am convinced that Oriente fired at his pursuers before he was shot. All of the glass could not have come from the small bullet hole in the rear window. I also believe that when Oriente's car climbed to the sidewalk and came to a stop against the fence, one of the assailants went to the front of Oriente's car and fired a shot into the man's chest and then took away Oriente's gun, which was missing when we reached the scene."

Police took Oriente's car to headquarters and searched it thoroughly for clues. They found only one bullet hole in the rear window. The bullet entered from the rear of Oriente's coach and then entered the back of his head near his left side.

Monmouth County Physician Dr. Harvey W. Hartman examined the body and found a hole about the size of a dime in the victim's head. There was no wound to his chest. Dr. Hartman said that Oriente died as a result of the single bullet wound but was unable to tell the type of weapon used. Police at first suspected the assailant had used a revolver, but after further investigation they determined that the bullet was fired by a high-powered shotgun from close range. They could not, however, determine if the killer was on foot or in a car. Hartman recovered the single steel-jacketed bullet.

Prosecutor Tumen assigned Special Investigator Crook to take charge, with help from County Detectives William S. Mustoe, Amerigo W. Sacco and Charles O. Davenport. Just a few weeks prior to Oriente's murder, newly appointed Prosecutor Tumen had asked Mustoe, Sacco and Davenport to resign their posts. Tumen wanted to appoint his own detectives. The detectives refused to leave and fought to preserve their jobs. Tumen instituted a strict new policy that each detective must account for his time and travel on a daily basis in writing and warned that infractions would be punishable.

This wasn't the first time that Salvatore Oriente had been the victim of an attack. Three years earlier, on April 18, 1927, Oriente was shot while walking home after closing his cigar and candy store at 814 Springwood Avenue. Mr. Leonard Megill, a widower of 1121 Springwood Avenue, witnessed the hit. He gave police a fair description of the shooter and details of the event. Megill was standing about three feet away and nearly in the line of fire. He told police a man got out of a car, put his foot on the curb and shot Oriente in his back with a sawed-off shotgun. "I turned when I heard the first shot," he said, "and no sooner had I done so than a second rang out. I saw Oriente stumble and reel about like a drunken man. His face was covered with blood. There seemed to be a big hole in it." The first round sprayed lead shot into Oriente's backside, from his shoulder blades to his ankles. Oriente turned and took the second shot in the face. The shooting occurred at 8:15 p.m. When questioned about the shooting, Oriente claimed he didn't know his assailant or the motive for the attack. Chief Horace L. Byram doubted his story, but Oriente held fast. Oriente survived this first shooting but lost vision in his left eye.

Asbury Park Press, *April 18, 1930.*

Detective Crook agreed with Captain Williams's theory that Oriente was put "on the spot" by gangsters in a turf war. They believed a truce had been called after the first shooting three years ago but that Oriente had recently violated the truce. A detailed analysis of the crime scene lent support to their belief that Oriente was ambushed. Detectives reconstructed a possible scenario: as Oriente was driving west on Bangs Avenue, he noticed someone following him. When he figured out what was about to happen, he tried to get away by turning south onto Dewitt Avenue, but his assailant was too quick and too accurate. Police think Oriente took a bullet to his head, lost control of his car as he tried to turn and then crashed.

At the time of his death, Oriente had been renting a room in the home of Mr. Paulo Caruso and his wife, Antoinette, at 71 Morris Avenue in Long Branch. Police questioned Mrs. Caruso about her boarder, but she said she knew nothing about him. "He only slept here," she said. "He ate all his meals in Asbury Park and never talked to anyone here about himself."

Detectives Crook and Mustoe searched Oriente's rented room and found papers that confirmed his illegal liquor dealings. They confiscated the entire contents of his personal belongings but would only reveal that they found two New York City newspapers, both of which contained stories of violent deaths. The newspapers were from 1922 and 1929. Police tried but were unable to link Oriente to any of the names in the stories. The May 26, 1929 edition of the *New York Times* carried a story about American gangster

Detective Harry B. Crook Sr. (1891–1973)

Al Capone, the infamous king of Chicago's gangland. Capone had just organized the machine-gun mowing down of seven members of a rival gang. It quickly became known as the Valentine's Day Massacre.

Police apprehended no fewer than five Italian immigrants as suspects in the Oriente hit, but all were eventually released. They arrested two suspects in Long Branch and three more in Asbury Park.

Less than twelve hours after Oriente's death, Asbury Park Detective Edward J. Burke arrested Salvatore "Chippie" Vivancio of Neptune Township. Vivancio, another Italian immigrant, was from the same town of Quindici, Italy, as was Oriente. About 1926, he was implicated in a manslaughter case in Neptune.

Detective Burke brought Vivancio to Asbury Park Police Headquarters, where Special Investigator Crook questioned him intensely for three hours. Vivancio was a short man with brown eyes and black hair. During his questioning, he wore a neatly pressed blue suit and a light tan hat. He admitted to knowing Oriente and told Crook he was looking to borrow fifty dollars from him at the time of his murder. He said he had borrowed money from Oriente several times before. Vivancio was an unemployed barber and an admitted bootlegger. When asked to explain his movements during the day in question, Vivancio told Crook that he had taken a train to Long Branch earlier that Thursday morning to express his sympathies to Oriente's family. Crook knew he was lying. Crook knew that Vivancio rode in a car with a friend to Long Branch and that he arrived there about noon. Mrs. Caruso confirmed that she saw Vivancio in Long Branch that day but said he did not offer any condolences and that he only lingered across the street from Oriente's apartment. Police held him as a suspect for further questioning and took him to Freehold.

Two days later in Freehold, on April 19, Chief Investigator Crook reinterviewed Vivancio. He grilled him with more questions for three more hours. His statements in Freehold conflicted with the statements he had given at Asbury Park Police Station two days earlier. Crook described Vivancio's answers as evasive. Each time Vivancio described his movements during the time of the crime, the detective heard a different story. "Vivancio's answers to questions yesterday were rambling," Chief Crook said. "Frequently he interspersed his replies regarding his movements on the night of the killing with 'I didn't see anyone,' or 'I was hanging around a barbershop,' and 'I was sleeping.'" The barbershop happened to be just one block away from the scene of the crime.

Crook was sure Vivancio was somehow involved and knew what happened. "We are convinced that Vivancio is lying to us in the statements he made in connection with the murder," he told reporters. "He is evidently afraid to tell us anything for fear he will be put on the spot." Prosecutor Tumen ordered Vivancio held as a material witness on $10,000 bail. Unable to post bond, Vivancio, or "Chippie" as his bootlegging acquaintances called him, was locked up in the county jail.

On April 18, Captain Williams brought Stefano Vacchiano in for questioning. Vacchiano was a forty-three-year-old Italian immigrant from Camposano, Italy. Vacchiano also was no stranger to the police. Four years earlier, he pleaded guilty to illegal sale and possession of liquor. For that offense, he was fined $150 and put on two years' probation. About ten years earlier, Vacchiano was implicated in a shooting affray. Detectives brought him to Freehold for more questioning, but Vacchiano had an established alibi, which police were able to confirm, so they released him.

After an all-night siege of the house at 328 Chelsea Avenue in Long Branch, Chief Crook took custody of Thomas Dimello and brought him to Freehold for questioning. Dimello was the third suspect apprehended, after Vivancio and Vacchiano. After establishing an alibi that police confirmed, Dimello was released.

Four days after the killing, the case went cold. Authorities had no suspects in custody. Chief Crook told reporters, "The prosecutor's staff, aided by the Asbury Park Detective Bureau, is making every effort to clear up all the loose threads in the investigation. We are following out all leads continuously and will make every effort to apprehend the slayer." Since there is no time limit on prosecution for murder in the state of New Jersey, the murder of Salvatore Oriente remains an open case.

RAYMOND WADDLE MURDER

About a year after the Oriente case went cold, Crook investigated another murder. On March 31, 1931, Detective Crook arrested Louis Parker and James Bailey for the murder of Raymond Waddle in Atlantic Highlands. Waddle died on the stormy night of January 5, when the three men were on a twenty-foot motorboat in the Shrewsbury River. Parker and Bailey said Waddle had lost his balance and fell overboard. They tried to pull him back into the boat but couldn't hold on. The men circled the area looking to rescue Waddle, but they couldn't find him. They told police that their missing friend had drowned. Police held Parker and Bailey when Waddle disappeared, but they were released when police were unable to recover the body.

Two months later, Waddle's body floated up, and a fisherman found it. Dr. Harvey W. Hartman did an autopsy and discovered that Waddle died from a fractured skull caused by a blow to the head. Hartman's autopsy revealed that Waddle was dead before he went into the water. Detective Crook arrested Parker and Bailey for murder. After twelve hours of grilling questions, Parker finally broke down and told Crook that he watched Bailey hit Waddle over the head with the motorboat engine's crank handle. Parker said the two were arguing over whiskey. Bailey denied ever hitting Waddle.

The jury found Parker not guilty of second-degree murder. He had taken the stand and denied his earlier signed confession, saying it was beaten out of him by county detectives.

CHIEF CROOK

On July 23, 1931, Prosecutor Tumen appointed Crook as chief detective. Crook's appointment caused resentment with some of the staff of detectives. Detective Felix Santangelo of Long Branch, a seven-year veteran of the detective force, argued that he was more qualified and brought suit. Santangelo was a World War I veteran who had done service overseas, whereas Crook served during the Mexican Expedition in 1912 as part of the National Guard. Santangelo claimed that Crook's duty did not qualify him for veteran preference, but the New Jersey Supreme Court upheld Tumen's selection.

On his promotion, Chief Crook made a statement to the press:

> *In accepting the position of chief county detective of Monmouth County, I fully realize all the responsibilities which go with the office. I will make every possible effort to serve the people of Monmouth County conscientiously and impartially. I sincerely appreciate the confidence in me of the prosecutor in appointing me from the civil service list and I wish to thank him and everyone else who has been kind enough to show any interest in my welfare in connection with the appointment. I also wish to extend my appreciation to the various police heads of the county who have cooperated with me during my service.*

Almost immediately, the public couldn't help but take notice of Chief Crook's daily routine and personal spending habits. He was publicly criticized for having his county-owned car washed twice a week at public expense. In

Detective Crook showing a photographer the three bullets removed from murder victim Al Lillien. *Courtesy Crook family.*

January 1932, Chief Crook married his second wife, Helen Manion, in Star of the Sea Church in Long Branch. The newlyweds spent their honeymoon on an eighteen-day cruise aboard the SS *Statendam* of the luxurious Holland America Cruise Line. They visited Havana, Nassau and Cristobal in the Panama Canal Zone.

In 1933, Chief Crook investigated the Alexander Lillien murder in Atlantic Highlands. Lillien's bodyguard, Walter Gerleit, and his gardener, William Feeney, came back from a business trip and told police they found Lillien's body lying in a room on the top floor of the old Oscar Hammerstein mansion, where Lillien ran his businesses. Lillien was shot in the head three times from behind. The murderers had left Lillien's body with a symbolic upturned playing card, the king of spades, and a pair of pallbearer's gloves. Lillien was the reputed mastermind of the Jersey Shore rumrunners during Prohibition. Chief Crook spent the whole day questioning Feeney and Gerleit, who told him they had no idea who might have done the shooting.

Spring Lake Teacup Poisoning

On March 14, 1934, Chief Crook arrested Robert C. Miller of Spring Lake for attempting to poison his pregnant wife. Miller lived with his wife, Elizabeth, and three children at 501 Ludlow Avenue. He was a wealthy builder and vice-commander of the Monmouth County American Legion. Miller asked a former employee of his, Edward Reilly of Eatontown, to buy a pound of cyanide for him. He told Reilly he needed it "to kill a couple dogs," so Reilly agreed. Reilly eventually admitted to buying the one-pound can of white powder for him at a drugstore in Allenhurst while Miller waited in the car. He paid $1.40 for the cyanide, made by Merck Pharmaceutical Company. Detective Crook believed Reilly was not involved any further but held him as a material witness.

Starting Thursday, March 8, Miller mixed a portion of cyanide into his pregnant wife's morning tea and personally served it to her with cream and sugar. He continued serving her cyanide-laced tea on Friday, Saturday and Sunday morning. That Sunday night, Elizabeth gave birth to a healthy baby girl named Marilyn.

Cyanide has a distinct burnt almond odor. When Mrs. Miller went to drink the toxic potion, she smelled a strange odor coming from her cup of tea. Mrs. Bessie Barker, her nurse, told her not to drink the beverage and put it aside. Nurse Barker poured the tea into a bottle and gave it to Dr. Robert Leighton, their family physician, while he was at the house checking on the expectant mother. Dr. Leighton tested the tea and determined that it contained cyanide. Nurse Barker told Elizabeth's

Principals In Tea Cup Poison Case

Here are the principals in the Spring Lake tea - cup poison case now attracting wide interest. Robert C. Miller, prominent 39 year old shore contractor and well known in county and state Legion circles, who is charged with attempting to murder his wife by putting poison in her tea as she lay in bed awaiting the birth of a child, is shown in the center in the dress uniform of a Legion officer. His wife, Mrs. Miller, who is recuperating from childbirth after having escaped death by poison, is seen at the right, and at left is shown Mrs. Mildred A. Conklin, typist and companion of Miller, who is being held at Freehold as a material witness.

Miller today admitted his friendship with Mrs. Conklin and said he discussed with her the quitting of her typist job.

Robert C. Miller in his American Legion uniform, arrested for attempting to poison his pregnant wife, Mrs. Elizabeth Miller, and his mistress, Mrs. Mildred Conklin. Long Branch Daily Record, *March 17, 1934.*

brother, Maxted Clinch of Lakewood, who reported to the police that Miller was trying to murder his wife. Clinch was the post commander of the Ocean County American Legion.

Thus began national coverage of an attempted murder in the sleepy little town of Spring Lake on the Jersey Shore. Residents of the community pretended nothing happened and were seemingly amazed at the attention this case got, with camera crews and reporters coming in from as far as New York and Philadelphia. Despite the national attention and several days of front-page headlines in nearby towns, editors of the local newspaper, the *Spring Lake Gazette,* also pretended it didn't happen. News of Miller's scandalous attempt to murder his wife by cyanide poisoning was glaringly omitted from the local newspaper, from beginning to end. Many said they were surprised at the accusations pointed at a man of such local prominence, although some admitted noticing that recently the couple was not getting along too well. Rumors had it that another woman was involved, but there is no mention of any of it in the *Gazette.*

Detective Crook went to the Millers' home and arrested him for attempted murder. Miller claimed he was innocent and asked his friends to keep an open mind. Miller said, "I hope my friends and the public in general will reserve judgment in this case until I have my day in court." He hired attorney Ward Kremer as counsel, who told reporters that "no poison appears in the system of Mrs. Miller." Justice of the Peace Fred Quinn ordered Miller held on $50,000 bail.

Crook also wanted to inspect the contents of a safe in the house, but after several hours, he and others were unable to unlock it. Crook told waiting reporters that he was looking for "something which has great bearing on the case" but failed to say anything further. The next day, safecracking expert Samuel Samuels opened the safe, and Crook examined its contents.

Crook answers reporters' questions in the Spring Lake Police Department the day after he arrested Robert Miller, March 15, 1934. *Courtesy Crook family.*

He didn't find any cyanide but instead found two "poisoned pen" letters addressed to Mrs. Robert C. Miller. Reporters surrounded Crook in the Spring Lake Police Headquarters, where he was hesitant to divulge any info about the letters.

"Were the letters of a poison pen origin?"

"They may be."

"Did the name of Mrs. Conklin appear in the letters?"

"No."

"Have you any knowledge of the author?"

"No."

"Did Mr. and Mrs. Miller have access to the safe?"

"I believe so."

Crook added, "We are prepared to work on the case all day, and will not leave until it has been solved."

Mrs. Mildred Conklin, a thirty-two-year-old attractive brunette, worked as a typist in Belmar. She was separated and lived alone from her husband. When Conklin heard that police wanted to question her, she turned herself in to County Prosecutor Tumen. Chief Crook questioned her at length regarding Miller's private life. She admitted being friendly with Miller.

Miller admitted being friendly with Conklin but maintained his innocence and claimed the letters found in the safe were blackmail. He said he had nothing to do with the letters, but Crook confiscated Miller's typewriter for comparison to the notes. Miller tried feebly to cast suspicion on others. From his jail cell he said, "Mrs. Barker, whom I have known for twenty years, showed animosity toward me lately, for a reason that I cannot disclose at this time." Miller smiled and said, "Every marriage has its rifts. We were not so unhappy as to provide justification for any suspicion like this, however. Recently my in-laws seemed very cold and never came to the house unless they knew in advance that I'd be away."

Chief Crook sent the cups of tea for analysis to Dr. Albert E. Edel Laboratories in Newark. Upon receiving the results, Crook told reporters, "The last cup, given her at noon Sunday, shortly before the birth of the girl, had sufficient cyanide in it to kill five persons."

Ten days after Miller's arrest, Edward Reilly finally came forward and talked to detectives. He said he had lingered because he feared the consequences of his actions. Reilly explained when, how and where he bought the cyanide for Miller. Chief Crook confirmed his story.

A few days later, Mrs. Miller told reporters that she had no disagreement with her husband and that they were not separated. "There has been no reconciliation because there never was a separation. The only time we were parted was when they arrested Robert and took me to the hospital." She said she was unaware of the plot to poison her. This remark differed from her previous statement, when she told Chief Crook that her nurse had prevented her from drinking the foul-smelling tea. Mrs. Miller testified briefly before the grand jury, as did her brother Clinch, but she refused to comment about her testimony.

Miller picked up his wife and newborn daughter at the hospital and brought them home, only to find reporters waiting for a statement. One asked him, "Does this mean a reconciliation?" Miller replied, "What do you think? We're here, aren't we?" Miller's attorney was thrilled at the reunion of husband and wife. Kremer said, "The developments, to say the least, have greatly weakened the state's case. Everything appears to be harmonious between the Millers, and after all, his wife is the person primarily concerned in the case."

The prosecutor's office wasn't buying the reconciliation. Prosecutor Tumen said they were proceeding with the charge against Miller. According to Section 111 of the New Jersey Crimes Act, "Any person who poisons or

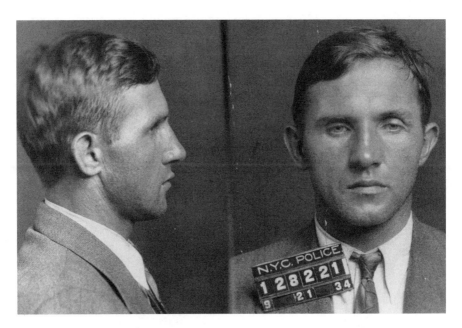

Bruno Hauptmann, convicted and electrocuted for kidnapping and murdering the baby of Charles Lindbergh. *Courtesy New Jersey State Police Museum.*

attempts to poison another with willful intent to kill, although death shall not ensue, shall be guilty of a high misdemeanor," and is subject to a fine of $1,000 or a jail term of fifteen years at hard labor or both.

This case never went to trial. In September, the grand jury found insufficient evidence to go after Miller. Eventually, the prosecutor dropped the charges and cancelled Miller's bail. Miller's attorney, Kremer, later sued Miller for nonpayment. The judge ruled in his favor, ordering Miller to pay him his $1,000 fee.

Crook also played a small role in the Lindbergh kidnapping investigation. In September 1934, he arrested James Barry of Howell Township as a material witness. Barry had been recently arrested in New York for attempted extortion and receiving stolen property. Crook accused Barry of hiring Bruno Hauptmann to build a house for him, but Barry steadfastly insisted that he had never seen Hauptmann.

$\mathcal{N}$aughright $\mathcal{I}$nvestigation

In 1934, New Jersey Assemblyman Theron McCampbell of Holmdel requested an investigation into illegal practices in the Monmouth County Prosecutor's Office. Assemblyman McCampbell sent a telegram to New Jersey Assembly Majority Leader W. Stanley Naughright, requesting Prosecutor Tumen's impeachment. McCampbell accused Tumen of a list of charges, including conniving with Chief Crook "to organize a spurious organization which attempted to collect tribute from speakeasies and disorderly houses."

As chairperson of the Special Investigative Committee, Naughright began to hold hearings on McCampbell's charges of political corruption and irregularities in the office. Convinced that something might be wrong, Naughright appointed Josiah H. Stryker to investigate charges of official misconduct in the prosecutor's office. Stryker looked into illegal gambling activities, protection paid, mishandling cases and misappropriation of funds, illegal slot machines, numbers running, gun permits to gangsters and more. Stryker said, "I am going to do the best I can. I shall follow this thing through with all the energy at my command." Naughright gave Stryker a broad scope of investigation to include any misconduct by any civil officer anywhere in the state of New Jersey.

In Monmouth County, Stryker interviewed the prosecutor, his assistant and the detectives. He subpoenaed witnesses and heard testimony from more than twenty local business owners who all claimed they paid for protection to continue operating illegal businesses locally. Stryker's findings confirmed McCampbell's accusations.

New Jersey Assemblyman Theron McCampbell of Holmdel called for an investigation of the prosecutor's office and for Prosecutor Tumen's impeachment. *Courtesy Red Bank Library Historic Photograph Collection.*

Editor George C. Hance published the entire, unedited report of the Naughright Committee's findings in the December 20, 1934 edition of the *Red Bank Register*. Its results were alarming. The report described the Monmouth County prosecutor's handling of some cases as "shocking" and referred to Tumen's actions in office as a "grave miscarriage of justice." The committee found Prosecutor Jonas Tumen guilty of gross negligence and misdemeanor of office and said that Tumen's actions merited impeachment.

Prosecutor Tumen was unable to explain some questionable circumstances in the conduct of his offices' employees. Crime prospered during his term in office, and he was known to spend lavishly. Justice Joseph B. Perskie removed Tumen from office and appointed Edward W. Currie as special prosecutor to

Detective Harry B. Crook Sr. (1891–1973)

New Jersey Assembly Leader W. Stanley Naughright established a committee to investigate illegal activities. *Courtesy Society of Free and Accepted Masons.*

immediately take Tumen's place. The Naughright Investigation also severely criticized the actions of Chief Harry B. Crook.

The report found that Crook did not properly account for money found in confiscated slot machines. Crook made a few small, occasional deposits of coins into Monmouth County bank accounts but failed to keep accurate records. On June 15, 1933, Crook deposited twenty-one dollars in silver coin into his own account with the Asbury Park National Bank. When Stryker asked the source of his deposit, Crook said, "I haven't the slightest idea."

When Crook arrested bookie and numbers runner Harry Taylor of Allenhurst, about thirty-four dollars was confiscated. Tumen could not account for the money and did not know where the money went. Crook replied, "That money is in a vault right across the street so that it won't be missing in the morning." The county clerk testified that the county did not have any vault in any bank across the street. On further investigation, the committee learned that what Crook meant was that he put the confiscated money into his own personal safe deposit box in the bank across the street.

Crook denied socializing with known criminals but was identified in a photo of the guests at Thomas Calandriello's wedding. Philip H. Phillips, another known gambler, was frequently seen with Crook at the dog track.

CROOK DISMISSED

Prosecutor Currie's first day on the job was January 3, 1935. Immediately, Currie met with Crook and advised him to resign or face charges brought against him. As Currie took over the department, he issued a statement: "I believe in fair play…Those upon whom I can rely on and who are not involved in the scandals will be retained. Fair play demands that our citizens be protected from transgressors…Chief Crook has been suspended. Unless he sees fit to resign, charges will be preferred in accordance with the conditions revealed by the Naughright Committee."

Chief Crook said he would fight his ousting. Crook had no intention of leaving, despite Prosecutor Currie's threat to file criminal charges, and told reporters, "I have no intention of resigning. Under the law, I am assured certain rights and I intend to stand on these. Furthermore, I am ready and willing at any time to answer any and all charges which may be preferred against me. For the time being, I am keeping myself available for the duties attendant upon the job of the chief of detectives."

Currie declared Crook dismissed, but even after his suspension, Crook reported to work as if nothing had happened. Currie gave him forty-eight hours to turn in his equipment. Finally, on January 7, Crook turned in his car, revolver, machine gun and ammunition but kept his detective badge. Crook hired attorney William George of Jersey City and promised to fight his ousting. He continued reporting to work a few more days, denying that he was legally dismissed. He said he believed that he was protected by civil service laws and that he was ready to answer any charges at any time.

Prosecutor Currie served Crook with an official notice of suspension, which automatically triggered a full investigation by the New Jersey Civil Service Commission. The notice charged Crook with incompetency, inefficiency and unlawful practices. Currie cited nine charges against Crook:

- Unfit and incompetent to work in the department;
- Neglectful of his duty;
- Unlawfully profited from his employment in the department;
- Guilty of conduct unbecoming an employee in public service;
- Converted and took for his own use money and property belonging to Monmouth County;
- Inefficient in the performance of his duty;
- Failed to pay and make reasonable provisions for payment of just debts, thereby causing scandal in the service;
- Had associated with those engaged in the violation of criminal laws;
- Made false claims in expense accounts filed.

Upon receiving the notice, Crook said, "The charges brought against me by Currie are without foundation and I intend to seek a full investigation of the matter before the State Civil Service Commission." His attorney filed a petition calling for an appeal of the notice of his removal from office. The hearing to appeal his suspension began that July.

Prosecutors brought in a parade of witnesses to the stand to show Crook's neglect. Witness George Hull testified that he was a partner with Crook's son John in operating the Lakeside Inn at Asbury Park. Hull said that Crook's father supplied the speakeasy with liquor.

Regarding the James Marson slaying on August 25, 1933, Highlands Police Officer Howard Monahan said that Crook failed to take fingerprints in the hotel room where Marson was staying. Officer Carl Parker arrested Howard Calandriello, but Crook allowed him to leave the building.

Prosecutors entered a photo into evidence. The photo was taken in the Molly Pitcher Hotel on October 30, 1932, at the wedding of Thomas Calandriello. A dapper Italian, Calandriello spent ninety days in jail for disorderly conduct. Recently, he had been indicted for breaking and entering at a railway express office. Mafia boss Vito Genovese of New York was his best man at his wedding. The photo showed that Crook consorted with known criminals. Crook explained his appearance as accidental.

Prosecutors entered Crook's bank accounts into evidence, showing that he deposited nearly triple the amount of his yearly salary in one year. Crook took the stand in his own defense. When asked how he could have deposited nearly $7,000 of silver coins in one year on a salary of $2,500, Crook responded, "I have no idea!" Tumen testified on his behalf, saying under oath that he trusted Crook and that he "had implicit faith and confidence" in him.

On September 26, the Civil Service Commission upheld Currie's decision to dismiss Crook. They opined that the testimony heard proved six of the nine charges against him, which was enough to justify his dismissal. The commission dismissed Crook's plea to overturn his suspension. Crook fired his lawyer and announced that he would appeal the commission's decision to the Supreme Court. He hired attorney Ward Kremer of Asbury Park, and so ended Crook's career as a detective.

POST-PROSECUTOR'S OFFICE

Crook found employment with the Coca-Cola Company, and the Red Bank Quadrangle Club asked him to be a guest speaker at its meeting. He accepted the invitation and chose to talk about vocational guidance.

In 1938, Crook was self-employed and living in Asbury Park with his second wife, Helen. He filed suit against Monmouth County in the Supreme Court to recover $2,800 in back wages.

WANTED FOR QUESTIONING

In 1944, former Detective Harry B. Crook was wanted for questioning about gun trafficking and for guns allegedly in his possession. New York District Attorney Frank J. Hogan asked Crook to appear before a New York grand jury without a court order. Crook agreed but did not show on June 20. The next day, Hogan called Crook's home. Mrs. Crook said her husband had been gone for about a week, whereabouts unknown, and she did not know when he would be back. Hogan saw Crook's action as evasive: "It is my opinion that Crook is evading questioning concerning his part in the transfer and disposition of guns."

On July 13, 1944, Judge John C. Giordano of Long Branch directed Crook to show cause why he should not be made to go to New York and answer the grand jury's questions.

Hogan believed that Crook purchased three guns from Asbury Park Police Sergeant Frank H. Rowland Jr. during the time Crook was chief detective in the Monmouth County Prosecutor's Office. Rowland had ordered guns from the George F. Herold Company, a licensed gunsmith dealer in New York City. Herold's records showed that Rowland bought three guns on January 31, 1933.

Records from the Colt Firearms Company in Hartford confirmed that one of these guns shipped to Rowland had previously been used in a New York double murder. On August 3, 1942, Max Fox used a .38-caliber Colt Detective Special to shoot and kill Robert R. Greene and Morris Wolensky

Detective Harry B. Crook Sr. (1891–1973)

Harry B. Crook Sr. with his eldest son, Harry B. Crook Jr., during World War II. Crook eventually sold his Armored Car business to his son. *Courtesy Crook family.*

at the Whitehouse Association and Bridge Club in New York. The serial number on the gun that Fox used matched one of Rowland's purchases.

Hogan wanted to know if the gun Crook purchased from Rowland was the gun used in the double murder. Hogan believed that Rowland purchased twenty-eight more guns over a five-year period and wanted to know Crook's involvement.

Crook showed up at the New York district attorney's office on July 19 but declined to sign a waiver of immunity for his immediate testimony. His refusal to testify before the grand jury put Hogan's inquiry into underworld gun trafficking on hold.

Harry Bernard Crook Sr. spent his waning years living in Avon-by-the-Sea at the Jersey Shore and wintering in Florida. He died September 7, 1973, in Avon and is buried in St. Catharine's Cemetery in Sea Girt. He was survived by his third wife, Ann Sullivan Crook. He was a veteran of the 1916 Mexican Expedition and a member of the Fort Lauderdale Elks, Avon Leisure Club and St. Elizabeth's Holy Name Society.

Appendix A
Monmouth County Detectives, 1892—1966

DETECTIVE	RANK	BORN–DIED	SERVICE
Strong, Charles E.	Detective	1838–1926	1892–1910
Norman, James	Detective	1853–unknown	1899–1899
Patterson, J. Frank	Detective	1855–1921	1899–1900
Rue, Jacob Bergen, Jr.	Chief	1873–1933	1904–1907
Minugh, Elwood	Chief	1864–unknown	1904–1914
McCormick, John L	Detective	1866–1957	1914–1919
Smith, John M., Sr.	Chief	1877–1945	1914–1934
Rue, Jacob Bergen, Jr.	Chief	1873–1933	1920–1925
Davenport, Charles O.	Detective	1866–1947	1921–1930
Santangelo, Felix R.	Detective	1893–1955	1924–1932
Shields, Leonard	Detective	1893–1938	1924–1936
Sacco, Amerigo Winfield	Chief	1893–1955	1924–1957
Mustoe, William Stanley	Captain	1890–1981	1926–1963
Crook, Harry Bernard	Chief	1893–1973	1930–1935
Kent, Merritt Bristol	Captain	1893–1969	1930–1966
Zuckerman, Harry	Detective	1895–1955	1932–1946
Tate, Charles	Chief Investigator	1885–1949	1935–1940
Woolley, Harold A.	Temporary Chief	1907–1974	1936–1940
Roberts, George	Chief Investigator	1883–1950	1941–1945
D'Angelis, John	Detective		1945–1945
Gawler, John M.	Chief	1913–1969	1946–1969
Green, John J.	Detective		1947–1966
Witt, Walter C., Jr.	Detective	1925–1994	1957–1959
McCormick, Albert V.	Detective	1913–1995	1957–1966

Appendix B
Monmouth County Prosecutors, 1828–2010

PROSECUTOR	PARTY	BORN–DIED	SERVICE
Lloyd, Corlies			1828–1833
Randolph, Joseph Fitz	Whig	1803–1873	1833–1837
Vredenburgh, Peter, Jr.		1805–1873	1837–1852
Parker, Joel	Democrat	1816–1899	1852–1857
McLean, Amzi C.	Republican	1817–1899	1857–1867
Allen, Robert J.	Republican	1824–1904	1867–1872
Conover, William H., Jr.	Democrat	1816–unknown	1872–1878
Lanning, John E.	Democrat	1840–1916	1878–1883
Haight, General Charles E.	Democrat	1846–1891	1883–1890
Ivins, Charles Henry	Democrat	1855–1914	1890–1897
Heisley, Wilbur A.	Republican	1858–1934	1897–1900
Foster, John E.	Republican	1864–1926	1900–1904
Nevius, Henry Martin	Republican	1841–1911	1904–1908
Applegate, John S., Jr.	Republican	1872–1950	1908–1914
Lawrence, Rulif V.	Democrat	1871–1938	1914–1916
Sexton, Charles Fletcher	Democrat	1877–1952	1916–1925
Quinn, John J.	Democrat	1893–1947	1925–1930
Tumen, H. Jonas	Republican	1890–1943	1930–1934
Currie, Edward William	Democrat	1896–1973	1935–1935
Bazley, Thomas Raymond	Republican	1885–1970	1935–1940
Quinn, John J.	Democrat	1893–1947	1940–1945
Carton, John Victor	Republican	1900–1982	1945–1955
Keuper, Vincent P.	Democrat	1902–1993	1955–1972
Coleman, James M., Jr.	Republican	1924–2008	1972–1977
Lehrer, Alexander D.	Democrat	1944–	1978–1983
Kaye, John A.	Republican	1943–	1983–2005
Valentin, Luis A.	Democrat	1966–	2005–

Appendix C
Rue Chronology

1873
September 12—born in Freehold, New Jersey

1878
family moved to new house built at 43 West Front Street in Red Bank

1885
March 19—father died in Jacksonville, Florida

1892
September 21—*Bennett v. Rue*

1893
August 1—married Anna Throckmorton Conover in Red Bank

1894
May 8—son Jacob B. Rue III born in Manhattan

1895
October 16—bought Stoutwood Stables
November 6—*Rue v. Knapp*

1896
January 16—fire destroys Stoutwood Stables
July 18—trained at Camp Sea Girt with Monmouth Troop, New Jersey National Guard
September 28—*Birdsall v. Rue*
October 1—*Holmes v. Rue*

1897
January 20—arrested for bribery
May 24—charged with assault and battery on Bodine
June 25—*Bodine v. Rue*, found not guilty
July 2—*State v. Rue*, convicted of conspiracy
July 21—arrested John Carroll for selling illegal liquor

1898
December 21—*Jones v. Rue*

1899
July 5—appointed Red Bank assistant marshal
November 15—arrested William Bullock for Walsh murder
November 18—testified at coroner's inquest for James Walsh

1901
appointed marshal of Red Bank
May 22—publicly criticized by Editor Cook for arresting bicyclers without lights
May 27—resigned as marshal

1904
May 18—appointed Red Bank chief of police
June 15—appointed Monmouth County detective
July 6—Editor John Cook praised Rue's actions
July—resigned as chief of police
August 2—reappointed chief of police
August 24—arrested Richard Byran for corner loafing
August 30—resigned second time as chief of police

1905
June 12—investigated Frank Rozzo murder
November 25—investigated William Brown drowning
December 17—arrested Howard Morris for murder of Mrs. Mary Naftal

1906
January 21—arrested Samuel Johnson for murdering his wife Henrietta
January 23—testified at coroner's inquest for Henrietta Johnson
May 14—captured murderer Edward Brown in Chicago

1907
January 5—investigated baby Callahan death
February—elected chief of Red Bank Bureau of New Jersey National Detective Agency
April 5—investigated Viola Bowers death
May 11—captured forger James Ayers in downtown Freehold
November 27—purchased Throckmorton properties

November 28—arrested Jimmy Sinicato in Catrambone murder
December 14—resigned as Monmouth County detective

1908
June 27—fire destroyed docks at Rue Boat Works

1910
October—leased boat works to Frederick Rumpf Jr.
October—leased docks to George and Forman Matthews
October—*Rue v. Mrs. Hazard*
October 5— purchased Frick Lyceum
October 24—opening play at Red Bank Theater

1911
April—joined Raritan Vigilance Society
May 21—arrested horse thieves

1912
August 30—private escort for Governor Woodrow Wilson at Monmouth County Fair

1916
December 6—formed private J.B. Rue Detective Agency

1917
April 25—hired to investigate poisoned pen letters to Mrs. Bewsick

1921
July 21—daughter Margaret married Bruce Campbell
August 21—investigated Mafia-ordered Camillo Caiazzo murder in Belmar
August 25—investigated John Woolley murder in Spring Lake

1922
July 24—shot in hand while recapturing James Ayers in Little Silver

1923
January 23—investigated Salvatore Santaniello murder
October 20—investigated bootleggers street gun battle in Highlands
December 12—son Jacob III married Grace Borden Conover

1924

December 18—investigated Paul Herry murder in Ocean Township

1926

December 12—retired as Monmouth County detective

1933

December 3—died of heart attack at home

Appendix D
Mustoe Chronology

1890

February 7—born in Brooklyn, New York

1908

July 15—arrested for illegal tree-trimming in Red Bank

1910

September 7—married Anna Sanborn of Red Bank

1911

April 17—daughter Thelma born
November 2—injured in fall off high ladder while repairing a streetlight

1913–1915

New Jersey National Guard, Troop B, Red Bank Cavalry, Chorus

1916

February—passed civil service test
March 2—first day on job as Red Bank police officer, at $840 per year

1926

June 23—appointed Monmouth County detective
June 30—resigned from police department
July—reelected president of the Red Bank Police Benevolent Association
July 1—first day as detective
August 6—investigated escaped leopard at Twin Brook Zoo
November 3—captured Clarence Tomlin

1927

March 6—investigated Rosina Stoble murder case in Red Bank

1928

August 12—investigated Max Turnow murder case in Keansburg

1929

January 23—got confession from fourteen-year-old murderer Belle Whitney

1930
April 30—refused politically motivated request to resign job

1931
March 31—testified at the trial of Lewis Parker for the murder of Ray Waddle

1932
March 8—traveled to Bedford, Pennsylvania, for Lindbergh kidnapping investigation
April 17—only daughter married George Nock

1933
February 1—daughter died of tuberculosis in Neptune

1934
January 10—appointed temporary chief of detectives

1936
January–March—assigned to Governor Hoffman on reopening Lindbergh kidnapping case

1945
February 8—appointed captain of detectives

1946
September 5—solved Elliot's Pavilion robbery case

1952
August—arrested Mrs. Ann Johnston for murder

1962
February 8—retired one day after his seventy-second birthday
February 13—replaced by Detective Merritt B. Kent
February 22—granted $3,830 yearly pension
April 27—fêted at testimonial dinner

1981
January 7—died in Pompano Beach, Florida

Appendix &
Crook Chronology

1891
October 20—born in New York City

1910–1917
served in the New York National Guard

1911
November 4—married Anna T. Harvey in Manhattan

1916
participated in Mexican Expedition

pre-1920
lived in Irvington, New Jersey, with wife and three sons, John J. b. 1912, Harry B. Jr. b. 1914, Edward T. b. 1917

1925
founded the Armored Car Service at the Jersey Shore

1929
January 27—wife committed suicide, family moved to Asbury Park

1930
April 1—appointed Monmouth County detective
April 16—investigated the Salvatore Oriente murder in Asbury Park

1931
July 24—appointed chief of detectives

1932
January 6—married second wife, Helen Manion, in Long Branch
January 7—began eighteen-day Caribbean cruise honeymoon
October 30—photographed at Thomas Calandriello's wedding

1933
March 23—investigated the Raymond Waddle murder in Atlantic Highlands

1934

March 21—arrested Robert C. Miller for attempted poisoning of his wife in Spring Lake

September 26—arrested James Barry of Howell in Lindbergh baby kidnapping case

1935

January 3—dismissed from chief detective job

January 7—handed in equipment

February 7—received notice of suspension citing nine charges of improper behavior

September 26—Civil Service Commission upheld suspension

October 3—filed appeal

1944

June 20—did not appear at New York grand jury investigation into gun sales to criminals

July 13—ordered to show cause

July 19—went to New York but refused to testify

1960s

wintered in Florida during retirement

1973

September 7—died at home in Avon-by-the-Sea, New Jersey

References

BOOKS

Ellis, Franklin. *History of Monmouth County, New Jersey*. Philadelphia: R.T. Peck & Co., 1885.

Gabrielan, Randall. *Red Bank Volume I, Images of America*. Charleston, SC: Arcadia Press, 1995.

————. *Red Bank Volume II, Images of America*. Charleston, SC: Arcadia Press, 1996.

————. *Red Bank Volume III, Images of America*. Charleston, SC: Arcadia Press, 1998.

Joynson, George. *Murders in Monmouth*. Charleston, SC: The History Press, 2007.

Ricord, Frederick W. *Biographical Encyclopedia of Successful Men of New Jersey*. N.p.: New Jersey Historical Publishing Company, 1896.

Taylor, C.W., Jr. *Bench And Bar of New Jersey*. San Francisco, CA: 1942.

NEWSPAPERS

Asbury Park Press
Freehold Transcript
Keyport Weekly
Long Branch Daily Record, March 1934

REFERENCES

Matawan Journal
Monmouth Democrat
Newark Evening News
New York Times
Red Bank Register, 1878–1962
Spring Lake Gazette, 1934
Trenton Times

PUBLIC SOURCES

Monmouth County Archives, Common Pleas
Monmouth County Archives, Coroner Inquests
Monmouth County Archives, Oyer and Terminer
Monmouth County Archives, Quarter Session Minutes
Monmouth County Historical Association
National Archives, Passports
National Archives, U.S. Census returns
New Jersey Archives, Marriage Licenses and Death Certificates
New Jersey Library, Governors' Papers
New Jersey State Police Museum
Red Bank Library Historic Photograph Collection
Rutgers University Alexander Library Microforms and Special Collections
Schindler Detective Agency Investigation Report
Smith College Archives

FAMILY DESCENDANTS

Crook family
Currie family
Hankinson family
Minugh family
Rue family
Vacchiano family
Wainwright family
Woolley family

Index

INDEX

About the Author

George Joynson is an alumnus of Bryant University of Smithfield, Rhode Island, and received his MBA from Fairleigh Dickinson University in Teaneck, New Jersey. Currently he is president of Holmdel Historical Society and serves as historian for Holmdel Township. An avid professional genealogy researcher, Joynson can be reached at gj@gjoynson.com.

Visit us at
www.historypress.net